Explore Your Sacred Truth

Explore Your Sacred Truth
A Quest for Finding Your Spiritual Reality

Theresa LePre

Epigraph Books
Rhinebeck, NY

Copyright © 2013 by Theresa LePre

All rights reserved. No part of this book may be used or reproduced in any manner without written permission from the author except in reviews and critical articles. Contact the publisher for information.

Book design: Bill McAllister
Cover Art: Ashok Nath Viswanath

Library of Congress Control Number:
ISBN: 978-1-936940-56-1
Epigraph Books
22 East Market Street Suite 304
Rhinebeck, NY 12572
Printed in the United States of America

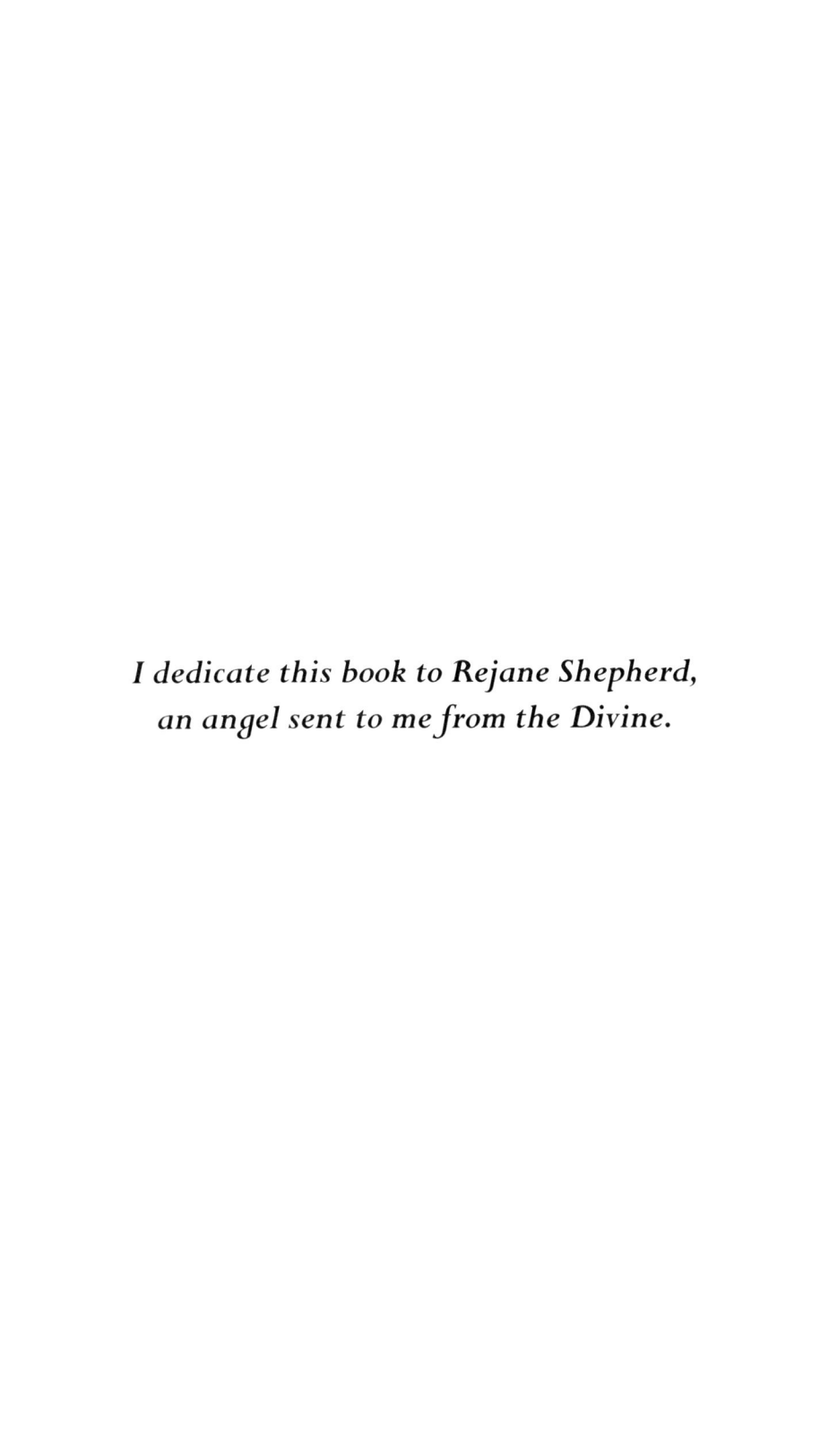

I dedicate this book to Rejane Shepherd, an angel sent to me from the Divine.

THE QUEST FOR YOUR SACRED REALITY

I would like to thank my family, who inspired me to live my purpose and gave me the opportunity to share my findings with others in the belief that they will find their inspiration to make a positive change. Jonathan and Shannon, whom I love unconditionally, may light shine on the two of you as you make your journey in this life. Most of all, my greatest inspiration, Chloe, my love, the sunshine of my life, who is teaching me how to see the world through the eyes of a child in its purest rays of light. Each of you has a piece of my heart. You are all gifted and unique, and I hope you see the beauty in yourselves as I see it in you. None of this would be possible without divine inspiration, for which I am eternally grateful.

Table of Contents

Introduction viii

Learning How the Senses Work 1

Living in the Present, Not in Illusion. 15

Living the Journey 27

Crossroads and the Ego Effect 46

Surrounding Influences that Impact Our Spiritual Journey 71

The Power of Communicating Divinely 96

Dimensional Energies and Your Spirit 110

The Mysterious Unknown and Understanding Its Spiritual Beauty . 124

Individuality and Spirituality 135

Consenting to the Journey. 148

Introduction

I felt an intense drive and urge to write about my spiritual journey that led to true discovery. It is my hope that those who read this are inspired to find their true life purpose and have the courage to live a life of fulfillment. The powers of universal law are very real, and when you are able to balance these elements, you open yourself up to a world of giving, understanding, and peace. This is when your true self shines, and it allows you to live in truth. Each of us has divine DNA, and when we learn what it is and how to use it for a better cause, there is nothing we cannot accomplish. When you eliminate the taunting voices of your ego and let vanity go, a solemn peace resonates through you, enabling you to reach your ultimate best. The light within you begins to shine and the universe starts to open up to you. In turn, you begin to understand that your life on Earth has a unique meaning. I invite you to share on a journey of self-truth. Use these fundamentals to help you find your true self. Mine was a bittersweet journey, at times thorny, other times velvety smooth; but very real, and it changed the way I live my life.

TL

1

Learning How the Senses Work

INTRODUCING SELF TO SPIRIT

IMAGINE WHAT THE world would be like if none of us ever questioned our existence. Questions such as, 'Why am I here?' or 'Who created the Earth and human beings?' would have no meaning, and we would never know our own spirituality. Fortunately, many sources of information have been recorded throughout history, and our natural inclination to believe in a superior Creator exists in our DNA. In recent years the need for inner fulfillment is a question that many people are seeking answers to. Many people are turning to the ways of ancient spirituality and are leaving behind the teachings of organized religion. The global economic meltdown, coupled with the loss of material possessions, has started a resurgence of spiritual re-evaluation, leaving many to ponder the question: Are my spiritual needs being met?

The most common reason why we begin to question our existence is because something is missing. At first glance, the only thing we are aware of is, that we are not completely whole. As we begin to dig deeper to the root of these feelings, we realize a strong need to fulfill our journey here on Earth, and that the things we have been doing up till now haven't met those needs. The quest to want to reach a higher level of consciousness, develop our individual spirituality, and improve in all areas of our life becomes an urgent need. A total shift in your consciousness is beginning to occur, and it is going to have an altering effect on the way you see things. At first these thoughts may rattle you because change means stepping away from the familiar. As you begin to make the transition from the old to the new, you must not let the fear of changing stop you from seeking the truth that can help you meet your needs.

Nagging, doubting thoughts that creep into your mind will most definitely try to dissuade you from moving forward. Thoughts such as: Am I entitled to the gifts the universe has to offer? Does a life of spiritual fulfillment really exist? Do I come from the same source of energy as the Creator? The list can go on endlessly if you let it. I understand all of them because I have experienced them, just as you will. It is normal to experience these feelings; when it happens, shake it off and continue onward. The rewards you will receive in doing so lead to living a life of abundance, in every sense of the word.

When I decided to write this book, I wanted to take an upfront approach with all of you and talk about what happens when you begin to transition. From this point onward, I would like each of you to think as if you are at the beginning stage of your life where you are going to effectively take advantage of the wisdom and knowledge you are acquiring, and put these lessons into practice, and use them to build a strong and stable foundation for yourself, one where you can be happy with the end results. This is the journey that leads to sacred truth.

Learning How to Expand Your Senses through Visualizations

As I sat down to write this book, I made a conscious decision to discuss many of the issues that are not usually addressed when people decide to make a spiritual change. Personal feelings and struggles that sometimes arise in the process cannot serve you if you don't understand them. I don't want to see any source of discouragement or temporary loss of direction cause you to give up. Having someone to guide you through the process is a reassuring point of reference for you, because it allows you to see that these things are common occurrences. Each of us goes through a stage where we feel like turning back; it is always so much easier to stay in our comfort zone. But when we know that we can find intelligent and logical answers to the questions we ask, we find that it is worth the effort for us to continue on the journey.

I have experienced days when I questioned myself; but deep inside of me, I knew that with patience and perseverance, if I continued to seek what I was looking for, I would find the answers. Through dedication and self-reflection, I kept striving to move forward, even when crucial crossroads were present in my life. The moment I was aware that I wasn't feeling balanced, I learned to bring myself back to center and realign myself with the Source energy that created me. You see, we share the same qualities that our Creator has. Once you surrender to the higher elements of universal law, all your discomforts tend to work themselves out. Let's begin with the visualization:

Everything that rises in your subconscious converges with your senses, establishing the basis of thought to manifestation. You are about to embark on a journey on which visuals, meditation, and connecting with your inner self all play a role in the exercises you are going to participate in. The three senses share an interdependent process, and learning how to use them teaches you to leave behind uncertainty, which will lead you to come successfully into self and spirit.

Explore Your Sacred Truth

Did you ever watch a movie on the big screen and become so captivated by it you visualized yourself playing the lead role? The desire became so intense that you created and set the stage in your mind, and you actually saw it happening. That is called visualization, and each of us has participated in it. That's the place we go to when we are alone with our thoughts. Referred to as the comfort zone in our mind, we can be anything we like when we are in this state and visualizing the possibilities. Everyone does it and it's familiar to all of us. I am going to show you how to use visualization as a tool to change your thinking patterns and help you better understand how to develop your spiritual side. By creating a positive thought pattern in your mind, you begin to change your thinking process into the reality you want to live. In short, the way you see things in your mind reflects how you respond to change. Keep in mind that you can use visualization for thinking through your position on a wide variety of issues that you want to change.

To get you started , I have developed a simple exercise that I want you to familiarize yourself with. In order to get the most from this exercise, I am going to ask that you follow a few simple steps. The first thing I ask is for you to find yourself a quiet spot. Next, clear your mind of the day's events and start with a blank canvas. When you are ready, I want you to begin with this breathing technique: Take slow, deep breaths in and out. As you begin to relax, you will notice that your mind is becoming clear and worry-free. The moment you reach your comfort zone, I want you to reflect on one thing that you would like to do in your lifetime and begin to visualize yourself doing it. Take this thought and nourish it in your mind. Set the stage and visualize yourself doing it until it becomes alive, and you see yourself accomplishing it. Stay in this place as long as you need to and

Learning How the Senses Work

let the intention set in. This exercise is the beginning process of manifestation, and it is the first step in how to form your visions into reality.

Planting the thought of what I call the seed principle is the first ingredient that encourages growth and prosperity. Using a diary when you begin is helpful and an excellent reference guide for referring to and seeing how much progress you are achieving as you make your journey. This is your personal memoir. Keeping a diary as you are transitioning will help you overcome any fear that you feel when beginning something new. There is an old saying that goes, "Fear holds you back from realizing your ideas." It's true, fear can be a deal-breaker; but not for long because you are going to learn how to control fear. In doing so, nothing will stop you from accomplishing anything you set out to do. Think of the power behind the words; it is essential you overcome any doubt that can block your progress. Once you let go of "fear," ideas take on new forms , allowing manifestation to take place, creating a new reality for you. There is no substitute when you want to improve in any area of your life.

Visualization helps you to understand the process of building strength from within and makes you stronger in all you set out to do. Once you master the technique, building a positive attitude and strengthening your inner core becomes easy. Acknowledge to yourself that you have all the necessary abilities within you to develop your spirituality and do all you ever wanted to achieve. Notice I said it's simple to do "once you master it." Realigning your way of thinking requires training your mind. And while you are in the process of doing this, you are in a rebirth. At times you might encounter difficult periods when you feel you are entering into uncharted waters; however, once you learn how to navigate the unknown, it is simple.

Explore Your Sacred Truth

Be aware that when you use visualization, action on your part takes place where your goals and dreams are in harmony with one another, and you'll be filled with vitality, enthusiasm, and a new energy. On this quest, keep in mind that you alone make the necessary changes in your life. You have guides that are always working in the background to assist you, but your free will allows you the choice to use your divine gifts or not. It all comes from you. Stay passionate about the things you want to do, because it is passion that keeps you motivated to create a difference in the things you want to change. If the road gets a little bumpy and doubt arises, never—and I mean never—let your passion diminish. Keep this thought in my mind, and say it everyday: I am on this Earth for a reason. I'm here to make a difference and live a life that has a purpose. When I teach, I tell people that a midlife re-fit happened to me. The time came for me to live my true destiny and do what I was destined to do!

Not everyone is going to agree with the new you. Those that don't, wish them well on their journey and continue on yours. This is about you and the choices you're making, the ones that are leading you toward a lighter place where you can explore your soul from within. Yes, I said soul, because that's what we are, living energy. Each of us is capable of doing the impossible! Visualize all you want to do, keep training your mind, and you will attract what you want into your life. When you doubt what your mind can do, think of the monks in Tibet and how they train their minds to be in perfect harmony with their bodies. Mind, body, and soul are in perfect alignment with each other, flowing seamlessly, like water, in a perfect melody. What an awesome experience it is, to live in synch with the elements of self, and it is an example of what human beings are capable of doing!

By taking the lead in your existence, you will achieve true

balance in your life. Your newfound confidence will help you find the answers to the questions you have been asking and open a path on which your dreams can come true. Accept your feelings and dare to express your emotions! An enormous energy flows through you, where clarity and confidence will enlighten your mind. Embrace your feelings. This is a time when everything is working in synch, and it will help you to solve all your problems calmly and quietly. Remember, you are in the process of training your mind to enter a higher level of consciousness, and that takes a commitment on your part. The training you will be going through is a metamorphosis, so to speak; you are shedding the old and becoming a new you, a being that is whole and complete—the best you can be! This is why visualization is an important part of the process.

INTRODUCING THE WORLD OF MEDITATION

Meditation is a peaceful state of mind. When you are in a true meditative state you are in total relaxation, and your mind is free of psychological dependence on your ego. When you meditate there is no barrier between you and existence. Gnostic teaching describes meditation as an open doorway within the human being that opens the way to personal knowledge of a phenomenal nature. Through the scientific and practical technique of meditation, one no longer needs to believe in anything, one can know. They go on to say it is an exact science based on real and tangible energies that are natural to human beings. How can we achieve a higher level of spiritual enlightenment from meditation? For many, myself included, the biggest challenge is to quiet your mind. For the beginner, it can be quite daunting. As soon as you begin your meditation, your mind becomes filled with chatter. It's very typical and it happens to everyone, so don't think that there is something wrong with you. It's part of the process, and it will fade as time goes on. There is no reason to get discouraged. I want to encourage you and let you know that it's all part of the process, and you should not give up! Even the masters experience the noise at one point or another. I'm going to teach you a few techniques that help the transition go smoother so you eventually become one with it.

Meditation is the tool that provides entry to the different states of consciousness that anyone who chooses to do so can enter when they learn the steps. Ultimately, you want to open the door of your senses that are now dormant. I'll address what you should to do with candor. For me personally, it enabled me to use what I have learned to teach you and guide you through the steps for a smoother transition. Reaching a higher state of consciousness through meditation enables you to perceive and answer the questions you have with a clairvoyant perspective.

Now let's get to it and learn how to benefit from the wonderful world of meditation. Mediation is an ongoing process that refreshes your mind and awakens your consciousness. To learn how to use meditation does not require money or joining groups. What it requires is self-analysis and the willingness to believe that you are going to experience self-truth. Different cultures use hundreds of meditation methods. I am going to share a simple method with you, to get you started.

Before you begin this meditation, make the decision to sit down and devote the energy of your mind to the exercise. Do it when you know you will not be disturbed. Take a few minutes to relax and be sure you are in your comfort zone. When you are ready, close your eyes and begin to breathe with slow, deep breaths. Become aware of your breathing with each inhale and exhale. Keep your attention on your breathing. Withdraw your attention from thoughts about past or future events. Using the power of your mind, keep your attention on just your breath. If you become distracted, slowly bring your attention back to your breathing.

When you are comfortable with the breathing, turn your attention inward and find the stillness in your mind. Rest in the stillness. Don't worry if you find yourself thinking a lot. This is normal. In time you will gain the ability to become consistently quiet within yourself. Go with the experience and let your subconscious guide you. Try practicing this meditation once a day for about 15 to 20 minutes. Finding the stillness in your mind takes persistent practice. It can be challenging because total silence is foreign to our minds. Keep practicing, and in time you will master it.

This is an important step in your personal development. A new cycle is beginning, and it is a period of learning and introspection. A door of cosmic revelation is open to you. It is a time to live at your full potential with no fear. Meditation develops knowledge from within and gives you comprehensive direction when making important decisions. It will never fail you. It's a proactive choice on your part. When you act in a balanced way, you are holding the reigns tightly on the future, guaranteeing success in all the things that you do. I like to think of meditation as an appropriate relationship with oneself. Take a moment to think about it; it makes total sense. And it aligns the foundation for all the other relationships you have. Put into practice the art of meditation every day. By doing so, you will begin to notice things that were always present but were muted in the background. Meditation liberates your life force. The torch of understanding will be turned on, and a mutual respect for all life forms will take place.

I can write about meditation and share with you my discoveries. I can teach you simple methods to get you started; but the only way you'll experience the magnificent benefits of meditation is if you begin to do it yourself. Superior logic and intellect resonates in you when you meditate. Learn to understand the rules of meditation and you can move directly to your goal. Now that you are familiar with the basis of meditation, begin to put it into practice.

GETTING TO KNOW THE ESSENCE OF YOUR TRUE SELF

The infamous inner self—yes, you. I am referring to the essence of your true self, that is your soul, the pure energy that you're made of, the energy you possess that is kinetic. That's right, energy has motion the very same way cells generate tissue. When I discovered that the body and soul are different and began to understand the differences between the two, and saw the potential power the soul holds for each of us, I have to admit, I was in awe! After many years of searching for answers, I finally understood all that I was seeking was within me. That's when I began to explore how to make it work for me in a positive way, and now I want to teach it to you. Understanding the different ways each of the senses work, you begin to awaken each one. However, all the senses interconnect with each other; and when the three are in harmony together, they become a balanced scale. Combining them into union is the means to awaken your consciousness. By comprehending your true self, you can revolutionize your mind. You are gifted with these natural tools, and they can provide a great service to you.

The time I spend developing these tools and using them enlightens every aspect of my life. It leads to a zealous approach

Learning How the Senses Work

for how I receive the spiritual opportunities that continuously await me. In the beginning of the rebirthing process, the obstacle for most people is doubting what they can't see. Most of us grew up in traditional religious belief systems, and we were never taught about the divinity that is in our DNA—a living energy that makes up the substance of who we are.

Growing up I was taught, as many of us were, that my Creator and Source energy was a god that would cast the disobedient ones into hellfire. Because I had special gifts, which I wasn't fully aware of and didn't understand at the time, a guiding force kept leading me to believe otherwise. When the divinity within me started to call out to me, I began searching to find my truth and life's purpose. Seeking answers about what my purpose was on my journey, I instinctively knew that God is a Creator that wants humans to live a life with a purpose and be happy. What I personally don't believe in is the fear many organized religious groups teach instead of unity and divine purpose. The same energy that comes from the Source of creation that manifests all things into reality resides in us. This shocks people because they were taught that we are unworthy to share this quality with the Creator. When their consciousness is awakened, however, they tap into the divinity they have and see the truth. The majority of people let fear lead them, but it doesn't have to happen to you!

Discovery is a wonderful thing, like the twinkle of excitement and wonder in a child's eyes when they do something for the very first time; when they share that moment with you it's priceless. That is the best way I can describe the feeling you will have when you meet your innermost self for the first time. It's a moment of pure exhilaration. So how do we tap into our inner self with positive results? Simply listen to the stillness in yourself and learn to become one with it. As simply as I write it for you, that's how it will come to you.

Become the person you want to be, not the one who doesn't want to disappoint others or the one who ends up sacrificing their dreams or beliefs. Know that your higher consciousness speaks to you through your subconscious thoughts. It's your personal guide. Yes, you heard me correctly. I tell you the key is simply to listen from within. Quiet the chatter in your mind and focus from your core, and a revelation will happen to you. It's been there all along, in silence. You are now freeing it to live. When you learn how to harmonize with your inner self, all the unnecessary sacrifices that were made up to this point that postponed your real interests are no longer feared. Presently, your inner self is showing you how to use your knowledge and wisdom in the manner it was destined for. Any negative aspects that have been like a cloud overshadowing you are cast away from you. It's remarkable when you achieve this and you witness what happens to your being.

When I was transitioning, reading was a source of guidance for me, and it helped a great deal. An author that I admire is Dr. Wayne Dyer. In his book Excuses Begone!, he states when you begin to kiss excuses goodbye, live in the "now," and change your thinking habits, things start to change for the better. It's absolutely true! I want to share something I came across when I was doing research one day. There might be difficulties and uncertainties, however, perseverance to find the cause of obstacles will finally lead you to the expected success (author unknown). I realize that it's not always easy, and as I sit here and write, I am teaching you what I have learned and experienced to guide you in your transition; but to fully comprehend, it, you must live your experience. I experienced many uncertainties, but in my soul I knew that if I surrendered, I would learn, and then I could teach and answer the questions that weigh on people's minds. I learned how to trust that "voice" that is my inner self.

Learning How the Senses Work

As I was meditating one day, I had a divine revelation that told me to write this book. In the beginning I questioned it and put it off, until one day I surrendered to my calling, and I sat down and started to write. When I surrendered, the divine guidance that had been prodding me forward also gave me the inspiration to compose with little effort. In that moment, I knew I had found what I was destined to do. I would like you to give thought to this next phrase. It refers to the law of cause and effect: Every act or thought brings about a fruit, and each action entails a reaction. Such is true about your inner self. I spoke earlier about rebirth; discovering your inner self is the birthing process of your true self. Natural intuition begins to flow, guiding you into a newfound confidence and sense of self-assurance. As this happens to you, a process of letting go of fear and obstacles begins, and things that once exhausted your mind no longer control you.

As you begin to peel away the layers that hindered you, the best of you begins to come out of what was once tunnel vision. Precisely speaking, when you realize your inner self, you're connecting with the real you. The benefits in doing so are that you'll realize your spirituality; you'll have peace of mind; self-realization will awaken in you, allowing you to succeed in every area of your life; and the list goes on. One thing is certain: Your inner self is the person of your true being. Most importantly, your relationship with the Source energy of creation is real. Eastern cultures have practiced this way of life for centuries. It is only in recent years that Western culture has begun to adopt these principles. People are looking for a tangible connection with the Divine, where there is acceptance and love. They are seeking to become an olive branch in society rather than a prickly thorn. Many of us are seeking from within to find the answers to the questions we have, to help us understand our path. Traditional

Explore Your Sacred Truth

ways of worship no longer have the hold on our generation that they did on the ones before us. People are raising their voices and questioning the teachings that no longer hold real value for them. They are in search of a belief system that has a connection with the divine elements, and they want a real relationship with the Source energy that manifested creation.

The three senses that we discussed all contribute to the awakening process. Develop and use them as you would a magnet, to attract and influence the things you want out of your journey and the people that you want around you. As time passes you will become increasingly aware of the changes that are taking place within you. And you'll realize with each day that passes that you are the creator of your own story. Use these tools daily to manifest a better you. From this moment onward, I want you to let go of the past, not worry about the future, and live in the present. Cast doubt aside, surrender to the Source energy of creation, and watch the obstacles be removed from you and a new path be opened up to you. New levels of vibrational energy will be activated in your body, leaving you with a divine DNA that has clear and concise objectives. Taking the first step by pulling the reins back is the beginning of having control in your life. The rewards are a greater liberation of the mind, body, and soul, defining your inner self. You now have been provided with the blueprint of how these senses work, and the basis of starting your life's purpose.

Living in the Present, Not in Illusion

Seeing Clearly In the Moment

AS I WAS processing my thoughts for this chapter, I was in the moment with no perception in my mind of past or future events. The only thought I had was the here and now. I was totally absorbed in the present. This is the essential root in learning how to fully develop our individual human potential. Undoubtedly, what lies inside you, and learning to understand it and develop it, requires your mind to be in the present. In the modern era, people have become so absorbed in where they're going, they forget where they are. The ancients had knowledge of techniques for not letting the mind stray from where it should be; but as civilization moved forward and science took precedence, ancient wisdom was discarded.

Integrating living in the present in your life provides you with the knowledge of directly working with your consciousness. By allowing the opportunity of discovering what is seen beyond the "physical senses," you realize everything in life has a purpose. The moment you become aware that each process you go through can help you live a life that fulfills your proposed objectives, you can easily create new ideas. This is how you begin to understand that "spiritual growth" is the growth of your being.

Presently, the majority of people globally are off on a

tangent. Busy lifestyles, not enough time in the day, always worried about the future and what is to be, and so on, have left humanity on a near- collision course to a spiritual meltdown. If only each of us could stop and roll the film back to observe how critical things are becoming globally, slowing down and getting back to basics wouldn't seem like such a bad idea. The ancients knew that living in the present allows us to be the best people we can be; they understood that is the way to call forth our inner self, to guide us on both internal and external, cosmic levels.

The best way to stop being anxious and slow down is to use the meditation exercises you have been participating in and make a conscious effort to control any fast-paced thinking patterns. That's the beginning of the moment when you start to take back full control of your destiny. Start with one thing at a time and don't expect instant gratification from the results. That's one of the biggest downfalls to making change: We want it instantly. If it doesn't happen in a flash, we quit. Should you get overwhelmed, go back to the basics and use your senses to visualize yourself in a calm and relaxed state. Your soul will listen to your calling and bring you back to the present, calming your being so you can think clearly.

The biggest misconception people have in the rebirthing process is they forget they're undoing a lifetime of negative conditions. As you move to a better place, remember the alter ego will try to prey on you and use your negative thoughts against you to move you away from reaching spiritual harmony. As someone who understands it, I can objectively help you overcome it. By using the tools that are available to you, you will remove any obstacles standing in your way. There's nothing more terrifying than to think that we are the only ones that have these thoughts creep into our mind and "almost" allow them to inhibit our progress. You feel as if your senses are splitting apart, and there is an eternal battle between your thoughts and subconscious. Frightened of what will happen, you are at a loss for how to regain control. When that moment happens, I want you to say this to yourself: I am the Divine Source of who I am, I am one with creation, and my path is clear to reach my station in life. Say this mantra until you are at one with Nature.

Gradually, you will feel your vibrational energy rising, and you will begin to feel divine rhythm return to you. True happiness can only exist when we free our minds and surrender and conquer our external self, in the company of a supreme divine state. Constantly strive to keep your mind in a state of clarity; that will provide you with the stability needed to feed your human side. It enables you to meet the challenges of life. Scholars agree on all levels that the human mind is the most amazing and powerful creation of Nature. It is capable of powerful changes, healing old thought patterns, allowing you to find new ways to deal with the experiences in your life. By stepping into your true being, you are entering into the two truths of life.

Determining the Pillars of Truth

The first is the ultimate truth, that which is beyond conditioned life. The Absolute surpasses time, measurement, number, and weight. It is the "real being" in you, the Spirit that relates to the ultimate nature of all things. It is only available to you when your consciousness awakens; it has no bodily form; it understands all and is invisible in the consciousness. It is the connection of all life sources in this world and the universe.

Explore Your Sacred Truth

The second seems like a contradiction of the first; it's what we call reality or the conventional truth. This is our human side of the five senses. It is limited because we relate to and see things as small fractions of the whole. In this state we tend to contradict ourselves due to the ignorance of which we are not even aware. Only when consciousness is awakened can you see both ultimate and conventional truths. This is not new; Hindu culture has been aware of this for centuries. If we fail to understand these two truths and our perceptions, we will keep making mistakes.

In modern-day culture, we have recently reconnected to these ancient principles and are learning what it means to live in the present. This is the time when you are metaphorically stepping away from illusion and influencing your subconscious mind to liberation. Superior logic is releasing the constraints that the ego mind had over you and replacing that illusion with a useful vehicle by which you can live in truth in the conscious world. This is why there is much discussion about and exercises for controlling the mind, because this is what can connect the two dimensions of the two truths.

I call these stages of change that you will experience "portals" because each time you go through one, your consciousness aligns more closely with your higher self. This may not always be comfortable, but it is necessary. It is important to remember you are not alone on your spiritual journey. The strength and energy that you need will come to you. Form a foundation for yourself, and be conscious of every form of wisdom and peace of mind you are receiving. If you find yourself in conflict with your egoistic mind,, come back to awareness. Take full responsibility for your life and your spiritual well-being, and take time to connect daily with your inner self and guides. Expanding yourself in all areas not only benefits you, it frees you! How do you do this? You have to create goals that can change your life. Goals push you to exceed your limits because you want to reach them. They are a source of inspiration to move forward; they give you confidence that pushes you forward and helps you expand toward spiritual growth. They transcend the mind to achieve positive results, dissolving limitations.

Expanding Beyond What You See

Finally, as your mind expands you will see the visible changes manifesting all around you. You manage any task with ease and positivity. Now you have the ability to leave behind doubt, control fear of the mind, and win back life with confidence. New knowledge replaces the ignorance that kept you stagnant for so many years. Past images of what took place no longer exist. You are not worried about what is going to happen in the future. You are in full flow with the present. Trust in every step you are guided to take. You are acquiring new knowledge that will help you understand who your true spirit is.

Now that you have a complete understanding of how to train your mind to stay in the present, there will be an opening of the heart center. Divine will and your will are merging. Now you will see your path open in unexpected ways. The release of expressing all the things that once were hidden inside you sets free your inner being. Yin and yang are in balance. A pure connection is forming between your higher self and inner guidance, one that unfolds inside you in a divine way. Everything changes. The way you look at a flower or the velvety midnight sky takes on new meaning. Your eyes are unveiled and you can see things through your lens in their natural forms. A magnificent bliss washes through you, and your appreciation of the beauty that surrounds you is vivid. You think to yourself, I missed so much. Now I can see clearly. And you say to yourself, I deserve to feel bliss and happiness!

As I reflect back, I realize how many burdens I placed on myself. I used to think about what happened in the past, worry about where I would be in the future, and I never thought a second about the present moment I was in. As I embraced my true self and surrendered to divine law, I let go of the things that no longer served me. Now I never think about what happened in the past; it's over. I don't worry where I'll be in the future; I know I'll get there. I live at ease in real time, the moment I am in. I can't express enough to you how liberating it is!

Try this exercise for the next seven days, and by the end of it you will feel a lightness from within, guiding you to mindfulness: Start by thanking the universe and the Source Creator for the gift of life. Then say: The past holds no more worries for me, for it is no more; the future has not come, so I will not dwell on it; the present is now, and I will live fully in it. I affirm on this day to take control of the way I live. Set your intentions clearly, and by the third day, you will notice a shift occurring in your thinking.

You are entering the stage of self-realization. This state is where all mental needs are fulfilled and the actualization of potential takes place. Abraham Maslow explains it like this: Self-actualization is "the desire of self-fulfillment," namely, for the individual to become "actualized" into what they "potentially" are. By following your spiritual path, you are realizing your own potential and abilities as you are entering into your own spirit. Experiencing the revelation that "I" am one with divinity and "I" am all that creation manifested me to be allows me to be the author of my life, freeing me to become one with the Source of creation and all that the universe is offering. Countless people live their lives

Living in the Present, Not in Illusion

according to the teachings of the ancients, and when you speak to them about the change, they all are living fully.

RAISE THE SPIRIT OF SELF

When I am discussing spiritual ascension,, at some point I always ask the participants how they perceive themselves. Almost always it throws the participants for a loop because the first impulse is to answer the question from the "alter ego." That answer is meant to impress. As I go further into the conversation and ideas are exchanged, realization sets in with the participants that I am aiming to make them think about their human potential. That's when underlying fear begins to dissipate and the discussion takes on a new form. Each person begins to explore the question from within. And they begin to understand that self-realization is when they reach the level of self-fulfillment of their true self. One fails to realize we are born as spiritual beings, and spirituality is in our DNA. Many are not aware that when they were born they arrived as a "spiritual being." The majority of people believe spirituality has to be learned, that it is an acquired knowledge. Not so! At birth you already exist as a living spiritual soul. Through outside influences and conditioning, we are lead to believe the opposite of the statement.

What has happened throughout time is that many diversities have incorporated themselves into our beliefs. Essentially we don't measure the effects that they have on us. Self-exploration is necessary if we want to gain back our birthright, which is that "I am"' essentially the "One Life," and it is incarnated in "me": "I" am one with all life source. And it doesn't stop there. You have to continue to explore your true self in order to experience "yourself." This is the moment you are engulfed in true spiritual intelligence, and your "true spirit being" that you were born with lives again.

Mind, body, and the "true spirit" are again in connection as one with the Source of continuous life. Now you are in the spiritual realm of existence. This is not concept, but truth. Every religion discusses and adapts to some forms of these principles. They just pick and choose what they want to use. The realm of the Absolute, where everything just is and is One, has been taught since the ancients. It is nothing new. You are in the present and you are in full awareness. Your refuge is found; your life force is one with all forms of universal energy.

Without even thinking, you can do things in ways that just flow very naturally and seamlessly. You are in the present, and there is nothing standing between you and the Source of creation and all its offerings. Now is the time to be receptive to what the universe has to offer you. Everything has a place and meaning for each of us. This is a decisive time for you because the illusions are not present anymore. Fear has no place here! The universe and all its entities are one with you, and your existence is one with it. The connection between the universe and human beings is evident, and life for humans isn't meant just to exist; it is meant to expand continuously. You are a conscious, living, self-directed soul, one who is taking back control. And the first step toward doing it is to be in the present space and time.

Our lives are determined by us, not by the things that happen to us. We either embrace them and learn from our experiences or become victims of our circumstances. But there is no reason to let the latter happen to you. Because now you are experiencing the essence of existence. Your spirituality is in you, it has been there since birth. It is not connected to religion. I am talking about the divine DNA that lives in you. One that is designed for you and is unique to your being. Discussion and awareness of its existence allows you to learn how to awaken it. Take a moment to think of it this way: You are walking on a trail, and you have walked this path frequently. But today as you walk, you consciously take notice of all that surrounds you. You see a tree that has many leaves, and they all look the same from afar; but when you come closer to the tree, you notice that the shapes of the leaves and their colors are slightly different. Each is unique and distinct. Even though there is only a slight difference, it can be noticed. And when you look at the tree in its completeness, all of its components blend in complete harmony with one another. The same is true when you see yourself in the present and not in illusion. Each of us are slightly different; however, our divine DNA is the same.

Seeing clearly and living in the present makes you realize that you are a part of everything in existence. For many this is merely conceptual. Most people are seeking their independence and fail to see the connection between themselves and all that exists. The illusion is thinking that we are so clever, we alone created our independence, without any interdependent interaction. Truth be known, when you think about it, we really never do anything by ourselves. Yes, we make our choices, it is true, but these are always accompanied by the support of someone else, a group, or the world. This isn't by accident. This is due to the interdependent connection that is present in all life. It has a cause an effect that's not accidental. When you become aware of our interconnection with all living creation, that is the single moment that you are introduced to your new life.

WE ALL HAVE DIVINE DNA

Intuitively, I always knew it existed, although as a child, I couldn't define it; the premonition of a connection of all as

One was always present in my mind. So I went in search for it. I knew we humans have divinity stored in our DNA. The question became, how do I bring it forth in myself and then teach others how to do so? We all have heard the expression, "The truth will set you free." Well, living in the present and connecting with our true spiritual nature also sets you free. In order to achieve this, you must become flexible in your thinking. The "portal," as I call it, must open. The exercises in the previous chapter will help you reach what is called "the original purpose of humanity." Opening the door to the true reality provides personal well-being and wisdom, and is a major turning point for you. But most important, your willingness to allow it to happen will let the energy flow to you. Then everything else follows.

Suddenly, the right teachers and guides show up. You begin to think and do things in a rational and methodical way. You are thirsty for new knowledge and discoveries, and, for the first time, you see life through your own lens. Everybody has a different purpose to fulfill. By finding the elements that lead you to your spiritual growth, you destroy ignorance. The veil of illusion is replaced with understanding, knowledge, and wisdom.

Everybody has a different purpose to their journey. It's not always on a grand scale and it's certainly not about material wealth. It has to do with the contributions you can make that make a difference. It could be as simple as bringing a smile to someone's face, or as grand as making world changes for the betterment of humanity. If you choose to live in full synch with higher universal laws, ask the universe to send you vibrational energies that will guide you. By asking, you will receive the guidance you need. In order to reach this level, you will need to direct your strengths, to adapt to a conscious level which is different from your level now. To know you are aware of your own spirituality is very exhilarating and opens new doors to you.

Along the way, don't be afraid to make mistakes. They happen. There are many misconceptions on the subject. Yes, it is true that each of us has a divine DNA blueprint that resides in us; but we also are housed in a human body. If you make a mistake, bring yourself back to center and continue on your path. It's that simple. Spirit is cultivating Itself in you, and you have to experience each part of the journey. This is the time that you are letting go of fear, unfulfilled desires, the past. Your emotions are bound to be unsettling at times. Continue to seek the "true self" of your nature, and in a short time you'll realize that you are entering into oneness with your consciousness. Your body is just the temple; your soul is the creation.

Are you familiar with the term "universal law"? It means free will, providence, and time. Free will is the choice to do something or make a decision. Providence is the manifestation of divine care or direction. And time is infinite and continuous. When you live your life according to the teaching of universal law, you are adapting to new principles. It is an extraordinary upheaval to your life, one that leads you to take a new direction on life matters. Your spirit becomes strong and enlightened when you live this way. New visions spread before you, making you the raw material of all your achievements.

I feel and believe when you allow yourself the opportunity, nothing is unattainable. In learning how to explore the connections in how all these principles manifest, you have the opportunity to transform your way of thinking. Freely allow everything that is occurring to take shape and form. This approach will lead you to interconnect the complicity of Oneness, to that which is palpable and easy to adapt to.

Explore Your Sacred Truth

Think of these writings as a guide that shows you how to get started. Everything in creation is created in oneness of principle, even though it tends to look otherwise. My goal is to assist you in accessing what is already inside of you. Each day that you live in the present, you can determine what is waiting for you. Your actions are justified and coherent. Your level of spiritual successes will undoubtedly be drawn by extraordinary achievements. When you live this way illusions fade and the true soul stays in the present.

III

Living the Journey

Personal Reason Is a Choice

"**P**ERSONAL REASONING" REFERS to the private choice we make when considering various options that are presented to us, such as when a person decides to embark on a spiritual journey and find fulfillment in life. It is a choice that is aimed at the most intimate aspects of the person. When you decide to take the path that leads you into spiritual discovery, your subconscious is calling and directing you to make these changes. And it's leading you to visualize a life that is consistent with your ideas and thoughts. Your subconscious mind triggers your brain to begin the process, and your aspiring consciousness leads you to take personal care in the matter. Your soul calls out to you, telling you that your search for self-knowledge is going to serve you and connect you with your spiritual nature. Finally, you ask yourself the question: Where do I begin?

As you venture into the unknown, it's just like anything else you start for the first time. A wave of thoughts go through your mind. You might ask yourself: How do the visions I have in my head manifest in reality? Why is the universe offering this to me? More important, how am I going to integrate these teachings into my life? All valid questions, all of which you can surmount. Not to worry. When you start you are at the beginning, what I call the introduction stage. This is the time that you take in all that you are discovering. Enjoy the learning process and don't overwhelm yourself. The universe and all of its elements know what you need to continue on your journey, and they readily will supply it for you.

As you continue to progress and you meet with new experiences and challenges, everything that you are learning will act as your guide. The universe is there as a resource to support you as you are rebirthing. Becoming one with yourself brings a multitude of healing benefits to you. As your spiritual nature grows, so does your overall well-being and compassion. A renewal of energy and vitality washes over you. And the connection you are making with the Source of creation is helping you develop with the oneness that is in you and of all creation. Remarkable, the way our existence and creation is designed to work in perfection. It completely changes your life.

I would like to go into depth about visualization, meditation, and the rebirthing process. I introduced the overall principles to you in Part I and instructed you in how to use them. Now let's proceed with how they'll help you in the rebirthing process, how they'll help to transform you completely, becoming a continuous resource for you throughout your life.

I'll set the stage with a parable for better understanding. What we are about to do is expand the practice of visualization into different areas of your life.

Visualization is a mind exercise that we use to expand our thought process and to create an environment that we want to have. It is also used to help bring about change. Here is an example: You have a relationship that is precious to you but somewhat strained at the moment. Both of you are a bit stubborn, and you fear if you advance to make amends, you might be rejected. So you let fear stop you from going forward. You also realize that perhaps you didn't give this person the support they needed, and you would like to acknowledge it and change your behavior. Your conscious mind is debating back and forth—Should I, should I not? This current state of mind leaves you with no solution.

Today you are going to use visualization to help you grow in this relationship. Do you see where I am taking this? For this exercise, you will visualize that you can communicate without fear of the outcome, that you are open to listening to the other person's point of view; the relationship is precious, and you seek understanding and resolve to work through it (please note, you can apply this to any situation that needs work). Keep doing the exercise until you feel the unwanted energy that kept you stagnant release. As this happens fresh solutions will present themselves, changing your old way of thinking into a new one with optimistic thoughts. You are not only picturing a positive end result, you are allowing it to happen by opening your mind to a better way of doing things. You choose acceptance instead of judgment in this exercise, and you allow your true being to lead the way toward a solution. Anytime you get a feeling that is off-balance with your center core, take deep breaths, realign your thoughts, and come back to the basics of your true self.

Openness and invigorating cosmic plateaus are elevating you to a new level of spiritual revelation that will have a fundamental impact on the way you see things from now on. The practice of visualizing can improve and change any behavior that hinders your growth, as it strengthens your character. You are becoming a higher spiritual being, being transported to a tranquil place where you are respectful and wise in your human relationships.

One stage of your life is coming to an end, and you are entering a new cycle.

You can apply visualization to all things and contribute a positive difference to your life's path. As you practice these exercises, you are learning you can create a life rich in spirituality and personal development. Developing your senses heightens your spiritual awareness. I speak with different people from all walks of life, and it is common to hear them say they are intimidated by visualization practice. I say, "Why? You have been doing it all your life." I usually get a funny look. Without realizing it you have been practicing visualization every day of your life. All the thoughts that enter your mind are visualizations. Every day in your thought process, you are doing it, from the moment you think about the outfit you are going to buy and wear, or what to eat and picture in your mind how appetizing the pancakes you want to eat are. And when you sit down to put on the outfit or eat the pancakes that you visualized, the visualization becomes reality.

As you gain insight about how to use your inner tools to govern your aspirations, you are igniting and using your "alpha consciousness," the part of the brain where you access your dreams, ESP, visions, and guided imagery. You have the opportunity to change all your old life patterns into a new path under improved and adapted conditions. Use it as an intervention that can help you as you develop on your journey. The distinction should be clear in your mind that finding your spirituality is your personal quest. You are a responsible and independent person, and fulfilling your spiritual nourishment will lead you to peace, harmony, and purity of mind, body, and spirit.

The word "spirituality" in modern terminology has different meanings to different groups, and many today misuse the word and miss its true essence. Its true origin is the ultimate immaterial reality, an inner path that enables you to discover the essence of your true being. Its intention is for you to develop your inner life through the divine DNA you posses. It is oneness with the divine realm and all of creation. When you choose to live a life of spiritual enlightenment, you choose to live a larger reality, where you transcend and experience the nature of the world. The glimpse of light that moves through your being leads you into a world where you will be cradled in self-realization, to new discovery that helps free you from constraints.

In order to understand creation and all that resides in the divine realm, we must first understand ourselves. Many texts have been written on the subject with many points of view. But if we do not learn the function of our own psyche, how can we awaken our inner self? Since ancient times, mankind has been aware that we have a sacred connection with all that exists. It takes great faith on each individual's part to deal with phenomena that are "unseen." Those who are willing to utilize the tools they are born with can reach the tangible state that perceives the true nature of the human mind. Others that are resistant to the true nature of humans do not reach inner enlightenment. That is why we call it "universal," because when you open to receive such knowledge, you connect with the primal Source of Creation. You enter a place where your being is whole and complete.

Visualization sets the course to assist you with what has not yet come to pass in reality. When you practice it, you tap into a powerful inner focus that is rooted in self-realization. You begin to get a sense of direction for what steps you have to take. The process of learning how to develop the why and how of the mind begins. Undoubtedly, and without fear, you are now ready to accept the "unseen" world of the psyche, where the true self of your being is making the connection with the Creator and the omnipresent qualities that were given to you to use. This is your birthright.

Take it all in as you watch a complete makeover transform you. You will be adapting to a different consciousness level from the one you are used to, and your intellectual ability will soar. Your understanding of human comportment will increase considerably. The knowledge that you'll acquire will be abundant and will serve to enlighten you, making you grow in your way of seeing things and how you interact with people.

The reason why most people feel stagnant in areas they want to change is they don't know how to restructure their lives. They aren't aware of their oneness with creation and the power it holds for them. Simply put, you posses divine power. Once the link is understood between spirituality and your inner self nothing can prevent you from making the changes that are inevitable. Completely freeing yourself from negative vibrations means you have to be willing to explore yourself from within. "Explore" is a perfect word to use because as you search, you will discover many hidden treasures within you. Tremendous energy pushes the inner you to the surface, and you begin to chart the course for yourself. You might be temporarily taken aback by what you are experiencing because it isn't at all what you are used to feeling. Any conflicting vibes that you experience will soon be abandoned by you, replaced by a celestial optimism that will reside in you as you discover the meaning of ascending into oneness with God, creation, and all that exists.

Don't cheat yourself out of the ascension into light; it is your birthright! Ask yourself: What can possibly stop me from discovering the divine connection? Why would I not want to use the divine DNA that is blueprinted in me? It has too much to offer for you to ignore it. This is a connection that few people reach on this Earth, yet it is available to everyone on the planet. Being receptive to receiving it and discovering your own divine blueprint is the key. I said it to you before, and I'll keep reminding you that when you begin to experience it, you will never turn back. You have a direct link to the Creator and all that is in oneness with creation.

Please understand that we create the circumstances that surround our lives. In our old lives, we were not aware of any harm we were doing, and we were led into uncertainties. Not anymore! Your divine life has arrived! I would like you to be conscious that when you decide to surrender to divine awareness, vibrational energies will support you in the process and help influence change in the rebirthing period. Now is the time to submit your will to these energies and let them resonate through you. I can describe it to you, but the feeling is unique. The only way to know it is to live it yourself!

I would like to share a true part of my life with you that I usually keep private: I always knew that I was gifted, as far back as I can remember. I always saw things differently from my peers, and I instinctively knew that our existence is far greater than I had been led to believe. I had a celestial yearning that was always with me. I always felt divine but couldn't grasp it. I grew up with a traditional religious background, and I came from a single-parent household. My mother was a devoted and kind woman. Although life was difficult for her, she always had a smile on her face. I didn't pursue the study of universal law at that time because I was on a different course. I always kept it in the back of my mind and knew one day I would. I was granted a gift that allows me to guide and understand people beyond what can be seen. I didn't realize it at the time, that being a spiritual guide and healer would become my life's mission. Helping people develop their divine DNA and find their inner selves is very fulfilling for me. The funny thing is I was doing it all my life and I didn't realize it. It just kept calling out to me in various forms. Surrounding energies that were influencing and guiding me were actually preparing me for this.

Hear the Call of Your True Nature

To make a long story short, I used to work in another industry and my company went bankrupt. Not only was I devastated, but my dreams collapsed. I lost my financial stability. I wasn't in a good place. One day as I was talking to God, pouring my soul out to the divine Creator, I began to surrender to all that is one with creation. I began to hear my inner self tell me to write and teach what I have learned. I thought, "This can't be! And more importantly, I have never written a book before!" Not worrying about the outcome, I surrendered to my calling.

This became my personal reason for being. I want to share the knowledge I have acquired, and I want you to know that you have divine DNA within you too. You can develop your own divinity on this Earth. Use it for your own personal well-being and connecting with your inner self. People are re-discovering and using principles in their everyday lives in order to live in harmony with Creation. Through my faith and belief in the higher principles, I gained the strength I needed to create for myself what I want to do while I'm here on Earth. There is a beautiful song called "The Beauty Of Peace," from the book Beauty 1 by Nicole Gruber. I listen to this song at times before I meditate. There is a verse that translates to "discover the beauty of the moment, discover yourself." This verse has an extrasensory connection of meaning, of being one with yourself, the Creator, and all of Creation. When this happens to you for the first time, the experience is so overwhelmingly beautiful, describing it in words can't do justice to the feeling that resonates through you. I invite you to live and not just exist anymore!

When you apply the principles throughout this book in your daily life, you come to understand the higher connections of self and spirit, and your thought patterns excel to new dimensions. Studies and growing evidence conclude that connecting with your higher self and living a life of spirituality makes a well-balanced person. I for one have experienced this, and each day I continue to grow and expand. Remember, every day is a learning experience, and as each day passes, the wisdom you acquire will advance. It becomes a way of life, and in no time at all, communicating with your subconscious is a normal routine for you.

It's like peeling away the layers of an onion: each layer that you discard brings you closer to the true essence of the soul. You are realizing your capabilities and your divine nature with each passing day. Most importantly, you are establishing a real relationship between yourself, the Creator, and the universe. You are no longer following a blind existence; you are taking the lead in an interpersonal relationship with the universe. The experience will leave you satiated. Your ears are in tune with the calling you are receiving. Your senses are no longer deaf with the lack of knowledge you once had; you now fully interpret all that is presented to you. As you speak to your subconscious, you begin to hear the answers you seek to your questions.

This might seem odd at first. When you are in silence with your subconscious and you hear the answer to your question in your own voice, it can be a little freaky. But I assure you, the answers you are receiving are real, and don't, I repeat, don't let doubt cast a shadow over you. You are truly being guided by the "true self" of your person. I experienced the same odd feeling at first. You are saying to yourself, is this real, is my subconscious really talking back to me? But why do I hear my own voice? It is quite normal. When it happens it will be only for fleeting moment. Let it pass. I can assure you, what is taking place is quite real. To know it is to understand it and to become comfortable using it.

The awakening of your soul has begun! There are many guidebooks and groups that can be beneficial to you; but the simple truth is, in order for them to be beneficial to you, you must commit yourself to using the tools that you are born with. You have a unique relationship with Spirit, and the more you connect with your inner self, the more you will instinctively know that is the truth. With each day that passes, you are living in complete harmony with your higher self.

People in general are pressed on this Earth. Fast-paced living coupled with the pressures of everyday survival can leave a person overwhelmed. However, there is an antidote to ease the burdens. Learn to take the time you need to nourish your soul every day, to keep you in harmony with all of creation. Approaching your life this way gives you the backbone to address anything that comes your way with the ease of knowing there is a solution. Sometimes it is not what you plan, but it will always turn out for the best.

You took a leap of faith and became proactive in your life. The moment you acted, embracing the higher principles of universal law, you entered a new phase in your life. You made a commitment to yourself to live according to the laws of Nature and Creation. By living in such a way, you will be the raw material of your thoughts. You will have to learn to use all that you discover with compassion, especially towards others. Your visions are clear as you approach life's developments. In short, you are changing radically and very much to your advantage.

There is a saying that goes, to know the "true self" and feel "inner enlightenment" is to be in meditation! Ancient religions encouraged the use of meditation practice as a method to perceive and awaken the divine DNA that resides in each being. I mentioned in the previous chapter that it is used to awaken the divine essence that is dormant in us. Learning to control stillness of the mind from within is the most demanding task of meditation. This is going to take commitment and practice on your part. But the rewards are consequential. Meditation is an eternal process that is considered to be an "extended thought" or contemplation of spiritual reality.

I would like to guide you on how to use meditation in your spiritual growth and help you benefit and advance from it. The East has been practicing meditation for centuries, and it has become increasingly popular in the West in recent years. Scientists are now studying and evaluating the effects that meditation has on the people who practice it regularly. Results are proving positive. People who meditate daily experience an overall repose in their being. There are so many benefits when one meditates. Not only are you awakening your consciousness, you are reducing stress. You are calmer, and your overall well-being is generally better.

The goal of the practice is to turn inward. As with any exercise you do, find a place where you will not be distracted and you can be quiet. It is very important that you are comfortable when you are meditating. You'll need a point on which to focus your attention. Slowly start withdrawing inward. Focus on your breathing, become conscious of each inhale and exhale of your breathing. Breathe using your diaphragm, not your lungs. Keep your focus on your breathing, slowing it down with each breath you take, allowing yourself to be in the present. This is where you can discover precise and deeper levels of your mind. If your mind tends to get diverted, gently draw your attention back to your breathing, and begin again.

Now that you are comfortable with your breathing, turn inwards and find the stillness of your mind. Don't worry if you become distracted or find your thoughts drifting. This is normal. Over time you will have the capability to become still in your mind. You have just to keep practicing.

As time goes on, you can explore other meditation methods. There are many techniques, each with a distinct action and use. Beginning something new can be somewhat overwhelming because you don't know what to expect. As you become comfortable and more confident meditating, you will wonder how you ever lived without it! Meditation teaches you how to maintain balance in your everyday life. Your skills become sharper and your mind becomes alert and functions faster. Your spirit is renewed and all your senses are engaged in perfect synchronicity with each other. Having a responsible structure in your life is at your disposal. Meditation teaches you to tap into an intelligence that is inseparable from creation and the universe. You act with wisdom in the way you think and in your actions.

All that lies inward has always been there; it was just waiting for you to revive it. The reason we practice these rituals is because it is the very essence of how we discover full awareness and illumination. When you are armed with self-realization, you stay in the flow with the energies that bring out the best of you in your daily life. Meditation methods are effective, and they are the link for communicating with your subconscious mind.

Meditating along with visualization allows you to penetrate the place in your mind where the law of attraction exists. Each of us harnesses the power of our thoughts that can influence real outcomes in what we want to achieve.

Meditation is linked directly with the brain. A new study published in October 2011 by the National Academy of Sciences indicate people who are experienced meditators show less activity in the brain's default mode network, where the brain is not engaged in focused thought. To put it simply, these people focus less on negative thoughts. When this happens in your brain activity, you are showing the positive effects of mindfulness. Not only are you connecting with your spiritual self, but you are also becoming a nicer and calmer person. Simply put, your brain is being rewired. Your mind is being trained to focus on the present and not wander. Image-engaging areas of the brain that are rarely used are suddenly alive. Pressures that once overwhelmed you are now dealt with efficiently. We have all experienced what happens to our thought patterns when we stray in our thinking; our minds can become a jungle. Think of meditation as a reboot of the brain, where you enter into nothingness to clean out any impurities manifested in you and recharge your brain's network system. Positive effects begin to transmit in the mind. When you focus more clearly, you have a sense of self-worth. Knowing thyself sets your mind free! This is just one example of the positive effects meditation has on you.

By using these techniques, the connection between self-improvement and spirituality is undeniable. In my own use of meditation, a shift of focus began for me, and the way I approach my life is now in synchrony with my Creator and the universe. Meditation directs your attention and helps you develop positive brain waves. Engaging in the art of meditation modifies and nurtures your brain, allowing you to change previous patterns that were responsible for interfering with your progress.

Your instincts increase and become a strength for you, serving you as an ally in all the decisions you have to make. You are connected to an internal source of guidance that will serve and benefit you. Your perception becomes acutely fixed on the now, rather than on the future. Your life is influenced by the observations you make and not by what other people suggest to you. When you put these techniques into practice, any past afflictions that slowed your progress will begin to fade into the background. This is the moment your life changes.

Self-confidence and self-esteem are key factors when making improvements in your life, which is why visualizing and meditation play important roles in your journey. They help boost your morale. By committing yourself to doing these rituals routinely, you build up resistance to distractions that can cause unwanted behavioral patterns. The benefits of living a productive spiritual life should cancel out the fear of making the needed changes you are faced with. Think for a minute about how this endeavor will transform you. Making an exclusive choice for the good of your being can only lead to finding true happiness and balance. Choosing to live in the moment is like a sculpture, the mere presence of which fills you with awe.

As your intellect grows and you learn how to develop fully your true being, your insight increases and you see how your spiritual wellness and everyday life are linked. Nothing you set out to do cannot be accomplished. The two techniques signal your brain to take action, enriching your life. It is such a rewarding feeling to know you are accomplishing personal empowerment, better health, and completion of your projects. You have the power within you, and now you are using it!

Living the Journey

Did you ever notice that people with a bleak outlook are stagnant and do not make any effort to change their lives? They are always in a doubtful frame of mind, creating a blistering bubble around their aura. They are stuck and usually don't know where to begin. They seem lost. It is not because they can't tap into the Divine Spirit, because we all have divine DNA. They simply have a barrier up. Most people are unaware that they have divine DNA. This is why raising awareness of what we are capable of doing and how we are connected with Creation is key to developing our divine senses.

Everyone on this planet wants to be listened to. The same is true of divine nature: it is calling you so that you may hear it! It wants to guide you and help you make wise choices within your being. Divine nature wants to lead you to a place where you are consciously in tune with the higher principles of Nature. Each of us contributes to the universe, whether we are aware of it or not, and if the connection is right, the universe works in accordance with our needs. If you're reading this book, you have a personal interest in your spiritual wellness, and you want to be a person who is in harmony with what completes you as a person. You are actively taking back the reigns and deciding which direction you will go. I am only the guide who has been instructed to show you a new path that awaits you. Divine calling allows me to teach what I have learned to you.

You are unique and special, and you are entitled to use these divine qualities that are wired into you as the Creator intended. It's up to you to make use of the them; you alone hold the key to success on your journey. When you choose the path of enlightenment, the course of action you take becomes parallel to the journey you are on. You are moving in the same direction as the connection with yourself and your Creator. You are motivated to self-improve continuously, to be kinder, wiser, and the list goes on and on. You are never too old to start. I would rather live the last ten years of my life knowing what it is to connect with my higher self and Creator, than spend my last days wondering what it would have been like had I done it. Better to spend one day knowing your true capabilities than never knowing them at all! Your true self is the basis, and that leads you to live in the present with sound judgment. The faith you have in the connection you have with the Oneness of all Creation brings you to think in a logical manner and use sound judgment.

The deepest aspirations of your soul are alive and in conjunction with the surrounding natural elements. Each level you advance to is a step closer to sacred truth. You no longer act in a manner that blinds you; past actions of uncertainty are replaced with an intellectual attainment that creates a good balance between your thoughts and actions. Putting all this into action requires you to be in a stable state of mind. The way you cultivate what you are learning has everything to do with how far you take your spiritual growth. Being spiritually fed makes the mind stable, and when you are balanced you become immune to any desires that are not reconcilable with being a complete person. You see the beauty within yourself with your inner eyes. When you have a compete sense of being whole within you, nothing stops you from ascending to great heights.

It is refreshing to know that you can rely on your own judgment when confronting decisions that concern you, rather than being influenced by the opinions of others. Your being is important and invaluable to your Creator, and all the universe wants you to succeed in being in the natural balance for which life is intended. You are in oneness with all of Creation. You and I were not put here to suffer unnecessarily. People can get caught up in uncertainty; we have forgotten the principles that are available to us. It is time to remember what the ancients have left for us to learn.

I engage in this lifestyle because if fulfills me and makes me feel in sync with the Creator and the universe. I use my intelligence and divine intuition to guide me. I have much more control over my life by living this way. I trust my inner self to guide me because I know that I am one with Spirit. I accomplish this a day at a time. I no longer have my ego gnawing at me. (We'll discuss ego in the next chapter.) I create an internal balance from within that transmits to the outer surface, and you can too. Look at this as an opportunity to create a privileged bond with your spirit. If your approach is serious, not only will you see the change happening, but also you'll feel it from within. It happens over time, in steps. It doesn't happen all at once. It's a steady growth, and you are becoming like a spiritual rock that is indestructible.

If you are still questioning yourself as to what all this means, simply think of it like this: Everything you are learning will enhance your intuition and guide you in a positive direction, all in a way that assists you in your exchanges in life. Think about that for a minute and absorb what it means. You'll feel your spirit being abundantly fed. Moving ahead you'll be living in self-realization and not self-doubt. You'll have come to understand what divine responsibility is, and each action you take will lead you towards a higher transcendental state. A deep satisfaction fills you as you live each day knowing that your potential is growing. Once you begin to evolve into your inner self, you learn to separate from your physical self, and your spiritual ideologies take form and grow. This is where all the hidden treasures of who you are live.

Explore Your Sacred Truth

Body, self, and spirit meet at the temple over which you are the spiritual master. This is how you learn ancient wisdom of the higher elements in a modern society. A spiritual evolution is taking place within you. If at times you find it difficult, keep your courage and faith and your thoughts positive. You will successfully surmount any challenges that appear. Focusing on your thoughts that are positive helps summon the energy you need to make all the things you want happen. You are capable of bringing forth your divine nature when you put a little devoted energy into yourself. This is how you use your mental power of manifestation. This is the reboot of your being, one that occurs over a period of time and lasts all the days of your life. It is available to you because it has always been a part of your DNA structure.

Everyone has divine DNA and can develop it if they choose to. Wishful thinking isn't enough. You have to commit to live in divine truth every day. This is how your senses become sharper and your ability to understand how the fundamentals of human philosophy develop and grow. It is an exhilarating feeling to cultivate meaningful relationships, both on a human and spiritual level. Living your life with no hesitation or doubt enhances your well-being. You will no longer waste your time or energy on situations that hinder your spiritual and personal development. Use meditation and visualization as an accent tool while tuning into your inner self. This will allow you to find the answers and solutions yourself without depending on others. You will begin to meet like-minded people who can offer valuable suggestions, rather than negative people who cloud the atmosphere. You can become a mentor to others who are seeking to find their true spiritual balance. You have the privilege of learning and using the ancient wisdom and teaching it to others who want to learn. It becomes a domino effect because it keeps going.

Living the Journey

In modern society many people are seeking a spiritual way to live in a world that has lost its way. I am teaching you how to get started. When you act to achieve positive results you are one step closer to reaching what was intended for all humanity. In most cases people create their own captivity by not advancing because it is easier to let someone else lead you than to lead yourself. I once temporarily had that mindset. I gave that way of thinking up a very long time ago and chose divinity. We all have a mechanism in us called free will, and we ultimately choose what we do. My free will pushed me to strive to be a better person and to become proactive for causes I believe in. I did this by letting go of my ego and facing the crossroads that I encountered along the way. I looked for solutions to the challenges that came my way. I learned how to temper my ego so that I could see with clarity.

IV

Crossroads and the Ego Effect

OVERCOMING ROADBLOCKS

SO YOU HAVE reached a roadblock and feel you are in a maze. The direction to take is undecided and you feel overwhelmed and stumped. Your ego mind is also trying to please itself. The two are in conflict with each other. You think, how do I overcome this setback and get back in step? Fear not, you are not alone. This happens to everyone at some point. In this chapter, I discuss how to overcome the effects of negativity that can occur during spiritual growth. I will guide you in navigating some of the crossroads you may face when you are rebirthing so you can take control of the reigns towards a positive outcome. You will learn how to overcome the fear that engulfs you when you reach a crossroads, and you will master the skill of tempering the ego mind. You will use natural-born intelligence to overcome obstacles in your path. And you will use the deepest convictions of your mind to control the ego. You will be able to act with a greater flexibility in your thought process applying these techniques when you find yourself off-balance.

A crossroads is a place where roads come together and then head off in different directions. We will use the word in a symbolic sense, and we will begin to understand that our spiritual growth is synonymous with a fork in the road. How we determine which path to take when faced with a challenge determines our growth. Here is an opportunity to overcome your fears and to use the full awareness of your mind to conquer the pitfalls that can happen. You are going to close the door forever on what I refer to as the "impostor complex," the false ego that causes you to spin out of control. It is a common mistake when embarking on a spiritual development journey to believe that when the decision is made to embark on divine awareness, the pieces magically fall into place. Some people think that if you don't reach enlightenment instantly, something is wrong.

Don't anticipate the worst. You may become tempted to take the path of least resistance and give up. All of us stumble on our journey at one point or another. That doesn't mean anything is wrong with you; it simply means that for a fleeting moment you are unclear and questioning your principles. Any number of situations can trigger this reaction in you. You may find yourself asking, is this journey worth taking? I am here to reassure you that it is, and brings with it enormous blessings to you. Effectively learning how to reason within yourself helps to control the chaos of the moment. Fear of failure makes it easier to give up and go back to unproductive habits that have kept you in darkness.

You are striving to be one with all creation. In order to attain wholeness, you must be yourself from the inside. Keep in mind that you have to be in constant awareness to achieve this state of mind. The ego is always lurking about and wants to be destructive. The good news is you are not going to let it take over and hinder your progress! You are in a state where you are fully aware of the present, and you are the driver on your course. Learning how to control the relentless forces in your mind becomes easier when you call on your divine DNA. Isn't that the most intelligent way to deal with any encumbrance?

Everyone has heard about the yin and yang effect. It is up to you to keep them balanced. Even when facing an obstacle, you can quickly stop the paralysis when you rely on your inner self for the answer and experience the benefits of moving forward versus the results of doing nothing. Quickly you will see when nothing is done there is a void; however, when you search for an alternative solution you have the potential to reach the desired goal. If everything were easy, how would you ever learn how to know yourself? There is no such thing as easy. We reach enlightenment by continuously using the tools that I discussed earlier. Rituals, such as meditation, visualization, and connecting with your inner self are programmed in us for a reason. They help you to use your internal knowledge in situations in life as we know it. You are a spiritual activist ready to take on challenges rather than cowering before them. The anxiety that you had is replaced with bravery and confidence: Bring it on, my divine self is here to help me. Tell yourself, I can handle what comes my way. My Creator and the gifts I was born with are my guiding source. Don't worry about the results, it will work itself out.

Beware on this spiritual journey because there are outside energies that seek to confuse you. These entities delight in doing so. They want you to turn back. Remember the yin and yang effect; positive and negative energies are very real. While you may experience fear at first, I will guide you in how to use your divine nature to combat it. First you must always remember you were created from a divine Source and you are armed with protection. The Source of Creation gave you the gift of free will, which is powerful and useful. Use your free will to conquer any fear that is placed in your path. At this point you are closer to your arrival than your starting point. Don't retreat because you become afraid. There is nothing to fear, whether you realize it or not. You have the tools, and they are your divine weapons against any attack that stands in your way. Negative energy fuels fear. When you learn how to control fear there is no more fuel to fire it.

If at this point you are saying to yourself, how do I control my fear? I say to you stay strong in your thinking, and call on your divine DNA to help you. You have a magical ability inside of you, and you were created in the image of the Creator and with the oneness of all of Creation on your side. Use it for good and its graciousness will follow you. There are some remarkable people who carry a special aura that can touch a soul with little effort. These people have a sense of understanding that spills over in all that they do. Most of these people have overcome great trials in their lives. The one thing that makes them stand out from everyone else is that they've always known that the powers of universal law are real and what they can do. They are seekers of ancient knowledge. They know reaching a higher level of understanding is their birthright.

You have it too, it is just waiting for you to energize it , I assure you it is within you! You have a right to it, it is not just for a select few; it is for anyone who desires to connect with the higher principles of the universe. Fortify your being with the knowledge that leads you to gain the secret wisdom that the ancients practiced. I have experienced all of what I am passing on to you. And I also had trials and tribulations along the way. So when at anytime you experience a flickering doubt, I want you to try this exercise:

Visualize yourself in a Zen garden. (Zen means to think about something and to arrive at contemplation). Visualize yourself in the garden. It is a place where you go to find logical answers and where peaceful and rational thought is generated . Let the

Explore Your Sacred Truth

vibrations you receive flow into you. When your mind becomes expansive, you begin to embrace the gifts that the Zen garden has to offer you. The purpose of this exercise is for you to be in the present and overcome confusion so you can deal with and free yourself from the problem. I use this ritual when I am faced with an obstacle or when I must make an important decision.

When resting in nothingness your inner self will give your mind a clear understanding of what you need to do. I say don't wait for a meltdown to have a breakthrough in your spiritual growth. As soon as doubt enters you, internally shift your focus and transform those thoughts into productive action. Truth be told, everyone has been in a situation where doubt is experienced. Remember, you are not indispensable; you are a divine being able to handle your life with vigor and vitality. Encountering a block is only temporary, and there is always a solution when you search for one. It's when you let it hinder you and stop you from proceeding forward that you lose out on living the divine.

There is no greater force than your own, especially when it merges in oneness with the Creator and the universe. While there are a select group of people who are assigned to be spiritual teachers and guides, without your willingness to seek and learn, how would you ever make the connection with Oneness? It is your conscious effort that advances the application by which the universe, Nature, and the living Source of energy manifests. Many people in today's society don't know the meaning of linking the energies from within because the practice has been forgotten. Instead they choose to be led by people who don't necessarily have their best interests at heart or do not know the way themselves. They put their fate into the hands of the unknown, leaving very few options to explore and an opening for a roadblock to take place.

Crossroads and the Ego Effect

When we fail to listen to our inner voice, we are tuning out what is being said to us by our most truthful and faithful guide, our divine self. No one ever said the journey was going to be easy, but I guarantee you it will be worth the effort. There is no greater gift than to love and reach spiritual freedom. Should you suffer a setback, you have the tools you need to help set yourself straight. As each day passes, the law of cause and effect will become more predominant in your life. You will gain personal satisfaction from being more audacious in your practice. There is not one being among us who cannot learn to confront life's challenges realistically and constructively.

This is your journey; live to the fullest extent where it is leading you. It is fair to say each one of us will face a trial in life; but by using your divine nature freely, you can place yourself in a better position to change useless behavior patterns. Become an antenna that is receiving the energies around you. I say this because when you are open to reap the gifts from life, the forces around you will channel them to you. Pay attention and do not waste time unnecessarily, because the sooner you find your inner self, the sooner full contemplation will begin to manifest in your life and you'll experience true happiness.

Contentment is what all people want. We yearn inside to have an overall sense of well-being and a true connection with Creation and the ones we love. Once you have it, everything else falls into place and doors will begin to open to you. Fear not the crossroads you might face because your faith in the matter will lead you to take action and arrive at your destination. I came across this quote, its author's name unknown. I thought it perfect for this chapter: "Understanding the deeper spiritual reason why you are living this experience, and allowing the possibility of a better future in you life, identifying what steps need to be taken

Explore Your Sacred Truth

and the decision made in a time of a challenge, and taking the courage to do what is called for in the situation knowing that divine help is with you." All this is within your reach. Think in steps, use meditation to calm yourself and think clearer, so you will be able to weigh the problem and find the solution. Listen to what your inner self is saying to you. Use visualization to manifest a picture in your mind of the outcome you want. Ask the divine energies that are with you to help thoughts flow into your conscious mind that give you sound answers.

You no longer have to suffer from debilitating thought patterns; you have learned constructive way of thinking. This is called growth because you are learning how to use the tools provided to you by Spirit and are being guided on your journey. We are all spiritual beings whether we admit it or not; deep inside we yearn for an intimate connection with Spirit and our inner self. That's what makes us feel complete. We want access to a better life. When you accept these revelations as truths, you will evolve continuously in every area of life. You'll adhere to new choices and a more promising way of doing things. When your mind is determined, your challenges become more tolerable because you have the tools you need to manage them.

Understanding Your Ego

The next crossroads each of us comes face-to-face with and no one escapes is the ever- temperamental ego. I am going to start off with this quote. Think about it and take a moment to absorb the words: The 'ego' is very fickle indeed and it is strong and obstinate. Oh yes, I am speaking of our alternate self, we all have one . The understanding of the ego can be confusing because of the vast variety of emotions it could stir up. It is at the center of our psyche and coordinates with our thoughts and our actions. If we are not careful with our ego and it becomes out of control, we have one big demon on our hands causing all kinds of problems. An out of control ego, will lead you into a entangled web that reaches the deepest caverns of our soul.

You might be asking yourself, why is she comparing the ego to a deep dark underground cave? Well, because your ego is anything but ordinary, and if it is unleashed and not managed it will lead you straight into the eye of a storm, one that leaves behind much damage. In today's modern society the ego is linked to the stories we read, but it isn't recognized as the problem. Although the word ego is not literally mentioned, it is at the center of what leads people to do certain things. Let's take a look at some of the ways the ego takes control of people. At the top of the list are vanity, greed, and pride. The display of excessive conceit is a common character trait that throughout history has caused many nations to fall.

Everyone wants to be admired, the desire is in all our hearts, and in truth we all have a competitive nature; but when the ego grows prideful, it goes out of control and brings destruction. To be so prideful that you think that you can do anything is acting without human regard. This way of thinking impedes positive growth and will not allow you to move forward in your spiritual or personal development. No matter who you are, at some point you will experience an ego trip. Thankfully there is no reason to panic because, as with all things, the ego can be contained. Your ego is not your true nature; it is what you create of it. When it becomes inflated one tends to believe all one's actions are justified.

We are going to learn how to understand the ego and use alternative measures to keep it within its boundaries. Freeing yourself of its ruthless effects takes discipline, but you will be a better person for doing so. What you should become aware of is that the ego gets to you in collective ways. Pride is famous for interfering with your growth if it is used in a negative way. I am not talking about the pride you feel when you have a sense of satisfaction from an accomplishment; I am speaking of when pride becomes a vice, when it manifests and creates such a high opinion of yourself in you that the "I" takes over.

When the "I" takes over, the ego falsely leads you to believe that everything is all about you; the ego doesn't have the ability to recognize itself and see the destructive effect it has. The ego is often associated with the mind and time. It is in constant thought about its future existence, not the present. This leads to obstacles and distorted thinking that takes control and impedes your growth. Because the ego has an impersonal nature in today's society, ego is quite the norm; the egotistical behavior of people is accepted in everyday life. A person's concern with "myself'" is always foremost on their mind. In order to learn how to balance your spiritual identity with your ego, you have to use your inner self to impose some control. The ultimate goal is to establish your "true self"; in turn, the results of your behavior will be consonant with your core values.

How do you reverse the bad habits of the ego into those that are positive? The first rule is you have to learn to think independently from the "I.". In order do this you have to develop a strong inner foundation that works in conjunction with your true self and conscious mind. By using the divine tools you have, your mind becomes a fortress of strength that controls the ego from spiraling out of control. Use the exercises that you've learned to help you. Your progress is already accelerating because you have a real desire to improve your lot.

Crossroads and the Ego Effect

When you begin to look inside and realize that you can go to your private space to gain access to your subconscious where there is no time, you can face your image. It no longer casts a false, egocentric reflection created by the "I." It becomes one with your true self, the one that bears witness to your divinity. Make use of the positive versus the negative to gain insight into how and what you are thinking in order to get rid of the harmful ego. You are now able to see below the surface and gain an understanding of what is taking place. This clears any negative energy that slows your progress because you no longer think in terms of the "I" and you cut the cord to the false ego. You will receive the guidance you need to continue on your journey.

In order to become aware of how to process this information successfully you have to become aware of the inner dialogue you have with yourself. This simply means to start talking to yourself kindly. I can hear you all asking, what does that have to do with ego? Here is the answer: When you use your consciousness to think with kindness towards yourself, it is easier to have kindness in your dealings with others. This tames the "I" in you and helps release compassion in yourself towards others. Set your intention to understand "your" ego, because its behavior is fickle, and when you know how your ego thinks it becomes easier to manage. You'll learn how to put things into the right perspective even when your ego is urging you to do something else . Keep in mind, the negative ego is not you; it is what the "I" creates. The good news is you can recreate the ego's intentions.

As you make positive shifts, your inner core begins to send signals to your brain, changing the ego to see the enlightenment that is in you. You are responsible for the change. You hold the power to change your thoughts and intentions, it's that simple! So as daunting as the ego is, you can control how it affects your actions and thoughts. Continue to be vigilant. You really do have the power within to understand your ego and keep it from harming your spiritual and personal growth. It does take effort; but once you do it, a free-flowing manifestation in the form of fulfillment starts to call to you.

Here is something to think about that will help you separate from the ego when you need to: When a child is born, it is born with no knowledge nor consciousness about its own ego. Notice the "I" doesn't control how a child acts. Children approach things with wonder and excitement, and they easily advance because nothing is standing in the way of their impulses. Learn to think from a child's standpoint and you will ascend to a higher consciousness, where there is no room for ego to invade and spread malicious thought in you. No doubt some experiences we go through are not comfortable; still, they are sometimes necessary for continued growth. Be mindful of everything that is happening on your journey, because it is your connection with your inner self, your Creator , the universe, and everything that is spiritual.

When you find yourself at a crossroads with your ego , the first thing I want you to do is to use meditation to come back to your center. Once you are at center, visualize a balanced and peaceful state of mind. This will harmonize your senses and allow awareness to take over. When you meditate, if you visualize and trust the true self to guide you, you will stay true to your principles and being. Difficulties are resolved more easily. The key is to focus on staying centered and in the present when you have a setback in order to rebalance your thinking and get it back on track. This is absolutely necessary when you feel that your ego is getting out of control! Otherwise, it will affect the way you think, causing your emotions and stress level to reach unhealthy heights. I spent much time learning and being guided on this topic. Use these suggestions as a guide to help you when you need counseling. They are in synch with everyday life.

1) Self Control When you decide that you are responsible for your actions and consciously become mindful of your thoughts , the "I" in you is no longer in control. To succeed in gaining control of your conscious thoughts, you have to be in a continual state of awareness. This is essential because your mind can be tricky and divert your consciousness. It takes effort to break away from unwanted and useless thinking patterns. When you feel yourself slipping, it is absolutely imperative that you bring yourself back to the present moment and back to center. When you feel balanced in your mind, you can take back control and put things in their proper perspective. This is how you contain the culprit that caused you to lose control in the first place.

Reaching enlightenment means that you also have to be compassionate in all your actions. Using your psychic strength and controlling your thoughts will help you accomplish this and make the change. Positive cultivation of your mind and practicing awareness helps you to achieve the transition. For those of you that are a little daunted about the effort that you have to apply, here is a mantra that you can use that will aid you: "I am in harmony with myself. I will use my intelligence to act each day in harmony with the present moment. I will remember that I am one with the Creator and the universe, and I will not let the false ego disturb the presence of my state of my mind." Our thoughts are a habit, and if you want to change old patterns that are useless to you, you have to do the work to bring a successful end to unwanted behavior.

Practicing love shows the fickle ego there is no place for it. The spiritual progress you are making is leading you to multidimensional stages, and you will radiate many levels of energies that will help you see things in a different way. Don't be afraid. Strangely enough this is what you should be doing. Be conscious of the things around you. Now is the time to be clear in what you want for yourself. Set your intentions and let life unfold as it should; this is a time when your thoughts will manifest quickly. Fear not, because the time has come for you to listen to your calling. You have the choice to control your being, your existence, and the center of who you are. This is your journey, and the subtle signs are all around you, guiding your every step.

When you take control and put things into order, you should be allowing positive energy to flow naturally from within. This is how you break away from mental habits that cause you to be motionless and make you feel you cannot achieve your goals. Awesome things begin to happen when you wake up from the inside out and you begin to open your eyes to see what is in front of you. The control I am speaking of is not forced, so that it makes you feel rigid. It is a released energy that allows you to take steps and build the confidence you need to accomplish a complete transformation.

Stop reacting and start observing all things that surround you. Replace old habits by openly giving and receiving love. By doing this you will know and understand what it means to have peace from within. Our life has a purpose. That is why it is important to learn the practice of meditating; it opens a portal to your psyche and awakens your senses. This is how the possibilities of what is available to you are activated. Look at is as a vehicle, one that is used in connecting you with your divinity.

Living in spiritual harmony, you become a positive thinker, you acquire knowledge, and you develop confidence, while being encompassed in love. What used to seem like the impossible suddenly is possible. You are in control of your life and are actively taking the steps to recondition yourself to new ideas that will continuously freshen your mind. This is called complete development of your subconscious potential. Everyone is born with this ability. I speak with such candor because you are entering a time when human will and divine will merge as one.

You may experience a mix of emotions as you transition. Be gentle with yourself; it is part of the process and natural to feel these sentiments. As you set the course toward change, you will begin to feel a great confidence inside your being. You will soon see the connection you have with everything that surrounds you. Whether it's your spirituality, relationships, Nature, or personal development, each plays a vital role in your life.

2) Inner Harmony All too often our minds are moving in many directions and the obvious answers to our problems are overlooked. The path to inner harmony is a journey that leads you to find and discover the beauty and peace that already exists in you. What you have to do is remove the obstacles from within and ask the question, who am I? Simply ask your true self to show you the way, and the answer will be provided to you. Think about that sentence for a minute and what it would be like to be in serenity with yourself!

Finding inner peace brings contentment, lasting friendships, and love into your existence, just to name a few of its benefits. It is a state in which all the senses are renewed. The feeling is very uplifting and healing, and it provides your soul with a state of calm. Inner harmony comes simply once you embrace your true self. Some people believe the true self creates it through a calm environment; still others believe you have to unite mind, body, and spirit. What has become clear to me over the years is that it doesn't matter how your inner self makes it happen, only that it does! Let your true self do the work for you; it will be happy to do so. Your vibrational energy will wake up a light in you and there will no longer be a conflict in you from the old ways.

Removing the unnecessary clutter from your mind will lead you to act in a consistent, harmonizing way that complements who you are. Without all the excess baggage and unwanted thinking patterns that the ego creates , you truly can develop the divine DNA that resides in you. You can benefit from living a life that dwells in harmony with Nature and the Oneness of all Creation, that the Source of energy has provided us with. Harmony brings with it the consideration of others and allows you to act with conscious effort, rather than a self-centered viewpoint.

Inner harmony is at the root of your emotions; it's the springboard that allows you to revel in your most cherished interactions with people. It helps you feel good about who you are and what you stand for. Begin by setting an emotional checklist for yourself; this will help you to process your thoughts about what direction you want to take in building your spiritual awareness, self-esteem, performance, and happiness. This is the general recipe to a strong foundation and happiness in your spiritual existence. After you have your checklist in place, commit yourself from this day forward to live by the values that are important to you. Through your actions and deeds you will feel harmony generating in you.

The effort is worth it and the rewards are abundant. The life you once knew doesn't exist any longer; unrest and anxiety are things of the past. It's all about the spiritual journey and living your life as it is intended, with a divine force driving you forward. Phil Jackson wrote this: "Keep an open mind and an open heart—the perfect advice when you are on a spiritual journey. This is why I keep reiterating to you to open yourself up to the energy that is there for you to use and benefit from. Watch the difference that it inevitably makes in your life! A calm and quiet energy will flow through you that will help you regain control of the mind, which can be quite active. When you find harmony within, you begin to live life in totality, and a soothing feeling resonates throughout your being.

The word ecstasy means the mental transport or rapture from the contemplation of divine things, a perfect description of how you feel when your being is in harmony with your inner self. By entering into a new state of mind, you discover you have a mentally divine conception of the way things should be. I was asked by the Divine to guide you in how to use what is already inside you, the capability that is and always has been in your DNA from birth. The next step is to use what you are learning in your everyday life. You have the exercises and the tools to begin.

Isn't it easier to go with the flow of the river instead of fighting your way upstream against the current? The same is true in your spiritual and personal development: Go with the streaming energy that flows like a current of water; it will lead you to your destination. It is a great experience to be in total harmony within your being; it is a time when you are in absolute agreement with yourself. Think of living in harmony in the present. It's the gateway that brings you to peace and allows you to align with your center core.

In order to achieve harmony you must learn to listen to your true self, and you will begin to understand your inner life. Then you will not be worried about the past or future, and you are able to live totally in the Now! When you reach this level, a feeling of deep gratitude manifests in your heart. You are free from worrying about things that have come to pass and you are released from anticipating what is to be! You are in perfect alignment with a consistent order, which I like to call a pleasing arrangement of self. Traits like agreement, congeniality, and amity all are working together. You receive satisfaction just knowing you are living in full awareness. In today's world, life is overly stressed and full of worries, creating dissatisfaction that casts a shadow over many people. By learning to be happy from within, we approach our daily concerns from spirit and light, and harmony follows of its own accord.

It's not a forced feeling; it is awareness mirroring the Creator's expression of how the human spirit is and how our visions shape our thoughts. When I think of harmony, this is how I perceive it: I envision a garden filled with love and peace, where I embrace a full understanding of what true birth means, birth that is the ultimate relationship with self, the Creator, and the universe. Everything surrounding me is lighter, my touch is gentle, laughter abounds, my very presence in the garden flows continuously like a garland of exotic flowers. Each soul on Earth is divine, and the first step in discovering your divinity is to listen from within.

To do this, find a place where you can be alone, sit quietly, and begin to still your mind. Listen carefully and you will begin to receive the messages that are being transmitted to you. As you listen, a gentle understanding begins to flow through you. Your senses are heightened and you attain a higher level of enlightenment. Take this time to transcend yourself and let your true being lead you to soothe away all the stresses and strains of everyday life. You are at the beginning of finding a truth and walking on your life's path. Be in agreement with all that happens to you, and harmony will follow. Believe these words I say to you now because they are said in truth. You can do and be anything you want to be on this earth!

Spiritual teachers agree that you have to grow from the inside out. It is said if you look inside, it will undoubtedly show on the outside. Learn to keep your thoughts simple, and positive results are imminent. The emotional and loving support that you need will find its way to you. By changing your thoughts and actions to expressions of unconditional love, they become consistent with the role you play on earth. This is the beginning of creating peace, love, and respect for all things. Become an instrument of awareness. Living this way will fill you with serenity, warmth, and true inner harmony. Placing you at an advantage , it will help to create balance in every aspect of your life. Remember, inner harmony is a beautiful manifestation of the spiritual life.

3) Understanding and Forgiving The French have a proverb: "To understand all is to forgive all." In a chaotic situation, you may not feel understanding; but understanding and forgiveness are the only ways to healing and living to your full potential. It is my opinion that there is a misconception of forgiveness. When you forgive, it doesn't mean you are letting the person who hurt you back in your life to hurt you again. It means that you forgive yourself enough to stop other people from hurting you, and you forgive the other person because you are not going to let hate fester in you. You can move forward without emotional baggage.

If you truly want to experience peace within, you have to be able to forgive. Humans have struggled with their emotions from the beginning of existence. If we express ourselves with raw emotion, the ego will unleash wicked harm to ourselves and those around us! Luckily we have evolved as a species into beings who have a higher thinking process and the ability to reason.

When you begin to understand all the surrounding factors that make up who you are, you are able to release the blocks within that cause difficult emotions.

Think of forgiveness as a temple of understanding in which your aim is to achieve peace with your fellow brother or sister. This approach allows you to comprehend a situation with empathy. In my years of listening to people from all walks of life and the different situations that they have endured, it is clear to me that all people want is to live in a harmonious environment. They want to have validated that what they believe is respected. In order to achieve forgiveness and understanding, the first lesson is to love yourself and come to term with the hurts you've suffered. Only then will you know how to understand yourself and others. This does not mean you have no backbone. It is the opposite; you are strong and in complete control.

Understanding is a psychological process related to a person, situation, or a message in which the mind grasps the idea of what is going on. It is built into all humans. I would like you to begin to expand your way of thinking and understanding by forgiving. In this way you are taking another step in evolving to oneness with all of Creation. The spiritual journey teaches us to think as well-rounded individuals. When you realize you have the power to connect your senses as one, you are more in control of your mind, your emotions, and the way you act. Reflect on this statement for a moment: Through you own willingness and acts of kindness to yourself and others you have given yourself permission to accept yourself for who you are, and you can use the surrounding energies to heal on all levels.

Recognizing your own authenticity as a spiritual being and seeing the beauty you have within weakens your negative ego! It no longer has any power over your thoughts. What you want to achieve is understanding through knowledge of your deepest innermost beliefs. You want to know yourself completely and understand yourself from the depths of your inner self. How can I do this? you might ask? Listen to what your inner self is saying to you as you meditate. This is a step that helps you to understand the true state of your being with clarity. There will always be spiritual forces in the background that help you . They may be hidden from your view, but by your allowing your true nature to flow freely, Spirit can help you to uncover what is inside you.

You will begin to notice that your thought process becomes clear, and that when you forgive it strengthens your spiritual armor. This is how you build trust from within and build up your relations with other people. As with anything else, it is about staying in the present and processing the experiences that enter your life. This is where your human will and your divine will merge, and it is the next step in your journey to enlightenment. As you are going through it, it's okay if your emotions feel a little overwhelming; it is all part of the process and it'll pass.

Nurture yourself at this time and accept your own intuition as a gift that guides you to understand your role on this planet. Face your day with the light that shines in you and the love that is within your heart. Look up and give thanks for your blessings and open yourself up to your true self. You are truly a beautiful being, and the universe is calling you to govern your spiritual prosperity. By expanding the way you think, you enter into a world that was once hidden from you. The time has come for you to embrace all the gifts that the Source of Creation is giving you. Act in kindness and respect, and the energy that is guiding you forward will direct you to a state of spiritual awakening.

You are cycling from the old to the new. You have all you need within to come to terms with past hurts that once weighed down your progress. You can do this because you have a new understanding of your presence here on Earth. You are gently coming to a place where your spirit guides are filtering new knowledge to you. At first the changes may be subtle, but they will transform you into a person who is able to process his/her thoughts with reason and stability. Little effort is needed on your part, because you are using your divine tools to accomplish the task at hand. Start creating the life you want by loving yourself first and then others. Believe you deserve it and it will come to you! You are the diamond in the lotus, and you are gradually transforming to a brilliance that is leading you to become an entirely different person. You not only have to experience the things in your own life, you have to feel what is happening around you as well in order to gain insight. This is called understanding and forgiving the human component.

4) Humility Humility is the virtue of knowing your true self as it is. To have it means you are respectful, grounded, and connected with godliness. It does not mean, as some people interpret it, being a doormat, groveling in front of others, or having less self-worth than the next person. In spirituality it means you are comfortable with who you are, and you walk with the Source of Creation and Spirit. Spiritual development means you are free from pride and arrogance. These are the essential features that are needed to become a whole and complete person. This would be a perfect time for you to think for a moment what humility means to you.

Humility is a quality that many people do not possess. There is a misconception about humble people. First, a humble person does not think less of him/herself. I have met many humble people who have accomplished amazing deeds in their lives; but they do not let vanity take over or advertise themselves. Instead they choose to keep developing their spiritual tools and using their resources to help others. People of this nature, what I call the self-fulfilled, they have God's signature on them and a deep acceptance of the human element. Humility is knowing who you are and not having the need for self-gratification.

People who possess humility instinctively know they have divine qualities, they know these qualities are their birthright; awareness is instilled in them. They're secure in knowing each person on Earth possesses these qualities and they respect the equality of human beings. They act as a dove instead of a raging bull. We all face adversities in life, they're part of the journey; but when you are secure knowing you have a relationship with the Creator , instinctively you know that things will work out. There is a light deep in you; it is cloudless and it makes you aware of who you are. We call it the connection of self and knowledge. You've made a choice to live a peaceful life and share the knowledge you learn along the way. I encourage you to search within because you possess the qualities we are discussing in this segment.

Keep these words imprinted in your, mind: Walk in peace among those who reside on Earth. The strength that is your being is a tower that stands tall in the sky, attracting many who want to know your secrets. A person who shows humility in the things they do knows these words are true. You'll be amazed how those who are knowledgeable and experienced will find their way to you and support will be offered to you. You become like a magnet, attracting what you need in your life at the time you need it. There are universal energies standing in the background waiting to come forward and help you. Be clear on what you truly want at this time; your thoughts are powerful. Most importantly, know that when you are conditioning your thoughts, the energy of the cosmos is manifesting them into reality.

There are many hidden answers that are all around you. I tell you to be mindful of your environment; you'll be able to pick p on the subtle signs that are the answers to your questions. Humility has no wants or needs; it simply knows you are one with the Creator and Creation. It is the negative ego that is dangerous; a wise person uses their sense and inner self to keep the ego in control . When you are on a journey that is spiritual, you learn that the physical and subconscious worlds are connected. Listen to the voice that is speaking to you from within. Do not muffle the words that are being said to you, for by hearing you will gain understanding. Keep this thought in your mind until your journey ends: Kindness brings understanding and true compassion to humanity.

5) Faith Faith and spirituality go hand and hand with one another. Each person's faith is different and has many facets; but the miraculous power it holds to the believer can alter their destiny. There are various interpretations of faith, but the simple truth is, when you posses it you act in a modest and respectful way. It takes on a life all its own, and the people who have experienced life-changing events against the odds relied on their faith and beliefs to guide them. They knew instinctively that they would be taken care of. Understanding that you acquire all things through your determination, dedication, and faith is the path that leads you to the infinite possibilities of what you can do. It is one of the key components in your path to self-realization and divine renewal. It is your birthright and you are entitled to it!

Crossroads and the Ego Effect

You play a very important role on this planet. It is true, at times we all travel a difficult path, and it is our faith that the Divine has a plan for us that carries us to a solution. Not for one moment should you doubt this. As I said in the first paragraph of this section, faith means different things to different people. Still, I believe we all can agree that the power of faith comes from our very core and without it we would live in despair. I am here to tell you that you are a unique and special soul, capable of having a life with meaning. Call on your faith when you face a crossroads or when your ego begins to lead you astray; your faith will help you out of a daunting situation. The belief you have in the Creator and the universe is a bond that no one can break. It will enthuse you in a positive way, as a reinforcement of hope, trust, and unmovable spiritual faith.

Don't let limited points of view stop you from developing spiritually. The stagnant period is over! Trust in the fact that you are being heard by the Divine and that you are actively taking the lead role in your existence. By using the divine tools you have at your disposal, you can take the initiative in working towards progress. I was blessed to have divine inspiration guide me; it allowed me to experience the blessing and also graced me to teach it to you. The help of guiding energies comes in many forms. The energy and spirit I have flow to me naturally. They give me the ability to teach at my full potential. Be mindful of using a gentle approach in all you do and you will find balance, more harmony, and the spiritual enlightenment you seek. Allow yourself to take the lead in your life and remember that we all face obstacles. By applying the principles of divine and universal law, you are learning to create new dynamics in your life.

Listen to your inner self and what you subconscious is telling you. You will begin to free yourself from many problems and burdens that try to enter your space. You will live within your true divinity and find the calling that is your destiny. Place your faith in the Source of Creation and you will see changes take place, and they will lead you to fulfill your destined journey! I would like to close with a thought for you to ponder: You must open yourself to love. First love yourself because you are important; then opening your heart to the other things that require your love comes with ease. The beauty of discovery awaits you!

V

Surrounding Influences that Impact Our Spiritual Journey

The Environment that Surrounds You

ARE YOU MENTALLY tied to your environment, the one that surrounds both the physical and etheric parts of your being? Most of us relate to the question, especially since we tend to do what we are used to. In this chapter you will use your surrounding environment to open your mind to new ways of looking at things. Learning how to access the hidden energies that are around you enlightens your spirit side. In order to reach the level where mind, body, and spirit come together, you must be willing to look beyond the veil and allow your mind to pass into fluid thoughts. What this means is you must learn to think in multiple dimensions, including those of the circumstances and conditions that encircle you, because all living and non-living things on the planet are subject to cause and effect.

The word environment in spirituality has a broad range of meanings. Let's begin with the human environment we live in and see why it is important to have a connection with those around you that is positive and supportive. Our human surroundings are those in which we affect and are affected by others. The best way to discover what is good for us is to step back and focus on how the most important people we interact with affect us. We must consider all relationships, whether they're platonic, intimate, or family, and how successful we are at keeping them healthy. How we approach these relationships is a crucial factor in determining the way we grow. This is true both when our relationships are harmonious and when we are not in synch with the people we are relating with. Mutual respect for the decisions each person makes is called adoration of our fellow beings.

With effort and openness you learn to develop your potential and see where it could lead. Once you begin to understand how Oneness and Creation affect you, you can see ahead. I am speaking of an environment where the human connections you have bring with them tolerance, compassion, and unconditional love at its highest level. I want you to reach a level where you can use spiritual channels so you don't regress in your thinking. The name by which you call the Source of everlasting energy isn't important; what's important is knowing that a metaphysical universe exists and you can tap into it. Don't subject yourself to anyone around you who could have a negative impact on your divine hard drive. When you meet opposition, keep your thoughts to yourself, and keep away from anyone who can negatively taint or influence your progress. Should you run across someone that is going to try and dissuade you, rather than argue, gently but firmly keep your ground and call on your divine DNA to take over. Your journey is yours alone. You will be sharing it with many others on the way; however, you must remember your path has to suit you! This is your life story and you have to see it through in the way that suits you, not them.

What people cannot understand, they fear! When we are frightened we tend to sacrifice what we want to do, instead of pursuing our beliefs. However, when we connect with the higher elements of universal law, they help us to eliminate the fear and make our relationships more successful. Having the

Surrounding Influences that Impact Our Spiritual Journey

capacity to love your Creator and yourself gives you the ability to regenerate your energy, so you can maintain it and make it grow within you. This comes from your environment, whether it is Nature, the cosmos, or people. Learning how to develop it leads to positive action and growth. People in general want to be part of a system that generates acceptance and comfort. We tend to follow the system for acceptance over anything else; most of the times people keep their true beliefs guarded. I'll give you an example. This is a true story:

I shop at a spiritual store in New York City. When you frequent a place, you get to the know the people who run it and you form relationships. On one occasion I was speaking to a member of the staff. As we were chatting , she told me many people who come to the shop don't share their spiritual beliefs or experiences with others because they are afraid that the others will think them odd. She told me when the economic crisis hit the shop was flooded with people from all walks of life. They were searching for guidance, not realizing they have access to their own spiritual DNA until they went searching for answers.

Some of those people I'm betting would never freely admit to others that they go to spiritual places to learn how to search from within. I was elated to hear this news because it confirmed what I always knew: The majority of people on this planet believe and receive vibrations from the spirit world, but fear speaking about it because they don't want to be labeled weird or loony. People are in search for a higher meaning to life and a way to make the connection with their spirituality. At some point over the course of centuries we humans disconnected from our true spiritual origins. Never feel odd about searching for your inner truth and life's balance. By taking a stand for these things you are expanding your thoughts and finding your true self. This is the essence that brings you closer to others and Creation on different spiritual plains. The person you were searching for from within is beginning to surface. Use the influences surrounding you wisely because they do have an impact on you.

Over the course of time change comes to each of us. Change is what we call a person's growth period; it continues until we leave the planet. The spiritual pilgrimage is the process of expanding our subconscious as we enter infinite dimensions; the experience is total oneness with Creation. You can feel the slightest vibrations and see the force of living things. What most people don't know is that each of us has the freedom to access this energy through interconnected frequencies that reach far into the galaxy. The Source of Creation has extended an invitation to you, one that allows you to evolve into your true self! You are free to progress in all matters with your guiding force leading the way.

Remember, not all the people you have relationships with believe as you do, nor do you necessarily believe as they do. This is where mutual respect for the other's belief system takes precedence and you firmly step back. Rarely do I encounter total resistance from another. When I do, I end the conversation humbly. Everyone has the choice to believe as they like.

My journey taught me many lessons. I learned how to confront the fears that were holding me back. Gifted people as well those who do not develop from within experience hurdles. What you are learning is powerful, and it is a gift that you must use with wisdom. When you enter on a spiritual road, there is no turning back. The experience revitalizes you. Your being is rejuvenated and your true self succeeds in all areas of life. To have a personal relationship with your Creator, your inner self, and Nature makes you feel you are living with purpose. That is why it is important to surround yourself with positive-thinking people, ones who encourage you to continue to evolve.

You'll come across people that are receptive to the same higher energies that you are, and a conversation will evolve. I encourage you to welcome these conversations. Learn from one another and teach what you've learned to others when they ask. One small gesture on your part may be a life- changing experience for someone else. We all have free -will to choose what we want to do. There is not a person on this planet who doesn't want to be loved and heard. This is true of all cultures on this planet. People are looking to make the spiritual connection. The relationships to our encoded divinity are as diverse as the people on this planet, and the learning experience is very real . Through patience and perseverance you will receive many blessings accompanied by wisdom. Feeling completely whole as a person and confident knowing that you share hidden knowledge with the forces of Nature enables you to live from your principles. My heart drops when I hear stories of people being afraid of having a relationship with their Creator because some traditions teach their followers to fear Creation. You were created in the image of the same energy that created all that exists. It has both masculine and feminine qualities.

Body and Spirit Your body is the host for your spirit; the two are separate from each other. Your mission is to find your spirit and develop it. Once you find your spirit, you will be led to discover great infinities affinities between your mind, soul, and Creator . These are the steps needed for true spiritual development. From this moment, move forward understanding the significance of the divine forces that are with you. You play a very important role on this planet, and when you are true to finding the path—or as some say, "the way"—divine guidance will lead you. I said it before and I'll say it again: Allow you spiritual DNA to flow. When I think about the gifts that we have and how divine guidance led me to write and teach, I am amazed! I didn't think it was part of the journey ten years ago. Throughout the bittersweet experiences I've encountered, I've been happy that I persisted in seeking and becoming receptive to my purpose. You can too!

I was guided to write this book, as the divine sources wanted it done. It may raise a few eyebrows, but as your logical self rationalizes the material, you will feel the harmony and truth it brings. The guidelines were written especially for you with help from the divine realms. When I compose, divine inspiration takes over and guides me as to what to write. I am sharing divine information the way Spirit wanted it interpreted to you. Each of us has a unique inscription encoded within us that was given to us to use. I am humbled that I was chosen to guide you. As you learn to unlock the metaphysical forces within you, you will use these energies of Nature as your steadfast guide. This is where it is important to keep your faith, especially in difficult circumstances. Difficulties happen, and resolving them is a natural process of life. Take this time to discover, question, live, learn, love, give, and receive, and continue to ask the Divine for help on your journey. The lens you are looking through holds a new way of seeing. I learned over the years in spiritual and personal development that people become very passionate about where the journey leads them. Each person's discovery is different, even though the lens they share is the same. Take advantage of this time to learn, be patient and tolerant of others, and mostly respect each other. When you act with spiritual judgment, you will always make the right decision.

I am sure many times you have heard the expression, "for the intention of good, extend the purity within your heart." When good energy starts to manifest through you, your heart does become pure. What it means is really simple: When a person does deeds and reacts to others from this stance, everything is done according to the laws of the elements of the universe. Your life balance is always steady. It is only when you let awareness drift that old habits try to infiltrate your space. One of my favorite expressions is, "The road to enlightenment has many avenues; however, we all arrive at our spiritual destination." Feed your true spirit nature abundantly through practice and sincere dedication; learn to develop your divine DNA. The dogma that divided people from the divine world no longer is affecting the relationship that people want to have with spirit. A large percentage of people worldwide believe in the spirit world, and they also believe it can have a positive effect on how we live. That is why those of us who believe are constantly practicing what we learn and are always seeking to learn more. Now I know that this may raise some eyebrows, but you cannot deny that it is true.

Humans have been spiritual beings since creation, and our divine DNA makes us aware that we are born with the need to have a relationship with the Divine. Globally, people are always searching to connect with their Creator. Many go on spiritual pilgrimages at some point in their lives. No question, everyone wants a better life. The next step is to invite the divine energies into your surroundings and welcome them into your life. And don't forget to embrace your inner child. This is important. Do as a child does: Embrace and learn to see things with pure intentions. When a child learns something new, they embrace it and they take in the whole experience. This is partly how you define your true self and its association with Creation. There are so many aspects of your surrounding environment that can have an impact on your life. You can draw from and utilize your surroundings to help you gain access to what is inside you. There are layers of revelations that surround you. Distinct visions will allow you to advance to new levels of understanding, Your spiritual awareness is heightened. Adopt all the principles you have learned into your life, and you will discover the love and compassion from the external and internal environments that you are a part of.

As you learn how to navigate the divine realm and live by its principles, you will be able to set an example to others through your actions and deeds. As you look around, you'll see clearly the workings of cause and effect, and you'll want to do your share to work towards a better humanity. As you reach this level, the words that come from your mouth will be filled with wisdom. You are taking into consideration everything that is part of your environment, and you realize everything has its significance to every other thing. The only thing that can hold you back is useless thoughts of your own mind and the minds of other people. Negativity or damaging thoughts are not part of your equation anymore! It takes a lot more energy to hold yourself back than it does to flow with the current. So stop listening to the voices that no longer serve a purpose for you. If they show up, immediately direct your thinking to Source energy and draw positive strength from it. In time, doubt will be replaced with the driving force of your true self. The past no longer plays a significant role on your journey.

Becoming Comfortable in Your Zone

Part of a healthy spiritual environment is a space that you can call your own. Find a place in your home that is your sanctuary,

Surrounding Influences that Impact Our Spiritual Journey

an environment that is peaceful, a place where you can be in tune with your thoughts and subconscious. Finding quiet could be simply a matter of closing the door in a room. I have a few spots around my home that I use as my spiritual environments. I meditate, connect with my inner self, and build my personal relationship with my Creator and guides. I take this time to get to know myself and the Source energy. I do this by speaking and receiving transmissions through my subconscious. You should try this too. The enormous amount of peace that flows through your body by incorporating these simple yet powerful steps into your routine is very soothing to your being.

Another part of your surrounding environment is practicing inner balance and learning the effects it has on you. I can hear all of you asking subconsciously, what does she mean? What I am conveying to you is that everything you do in your life has to be in balance with the universal elements in order to be in synch with the Oneness. You are always connected to Source and to divine love, wisdom, and intelligence. The majority of humans forget this connection, so they don't use it! People are always racing to go nowhere fast. Slow down. Speeding through life is why people swing from one extreme to another emotionally. Most folks do not enjoy human existence the way it was intended for our kind. This type of circuit overload exhausts our life force. In order to keep the scales in balance, we have to reach interior spiritual growth. In order to reach this stage, you have to go deep inside till you reach your core. Use meditation to assist you in reaching your core. Too much of one thing and not enough of another is not good for your soul. It is like recycling: You are releasing and taking in energy, always filtering it so it remains healthy. A good old cleanup discarding any negative energy that has built up and is hindering you is the perfect place to start. Practice going deep into your subconscious, and when you have a breakthrough, the answers will surface to your conscious mind as if they were laid out to you in a book. Living in an environment that has balance requires effort on your part because it is you that has to develop your divine side. The goal is to evolve into a higher being whose mind is learning new multidimensional ways of thinking. Balance in your life means molding yourself into the person you were meant to be. Exploring and finding out who you are—these are the fundamentals in becoming humanly complete and spiritually fed. This is why people are constantly striving to find a place of peace and acceptance among their peers while they are here.

I would like you to try this simple exercise in the environment where you live: Look at something that you see every day, but today look at it from your interior self. Notice how you begin to see every detail as if you are discovering it for the first time. Everything is pronounced; you see the smallest detail and are aware that everything is interconnected with everything else.

Becoming One with the Spiritual Environments

There are different elements that make up a spiritual environment, but they all work together according to divine law. You will feel your energy change within you; remember you are in a re-birthing period. As your spiritual frequency changes, your body will be in an adjustment cycle. This is the type of energy that you will receive from your environment. There are endless possibilities before you and no more predictability. When you began to understand how interior sight works, it will be easier for you use it to assist you on your journey. This is called well-spent energy, the kind that gives you aptitude to balance your full awareness. When you are in balance spiritually you can successfully cope with all the parameters of your life. There is no greater satisfaction than being inspired and inspiring. The Earth's environment is a true bounty in which to find knowledge. Everyone is searching for a Utopia on earth. What they fail to realize is, if they stop and absorb it all for a minute, all they seek is right in front of them. This is sacred truth. It lives in you in your divine DNA. As you grow you bring the things you are seeking to fruition. To maintain balance you have to draw on the resources within; this is the nourishing your soul needs to remain whole. In modern times people are taking a good look at their lives. We are ruled by the technological era, but with all our advancements this still cannot quench the need in people to search for a higher source. This information is based on fact. I have spent countless hours researching spiritual subject matters.

The questions that everyone asks themselves are, why do I exist, and what is my purpose? I have asked myself the same questions and most probably you have too! In modern society as we know it, more people are getting in touch with their spiritual side. People are discovering that the core values of spiritual teachings are based on ancient principles in which developing your divine DNA was taught and practiced openly. These teachings were encouraged and practiced throughout the community. Communities existed where people were spiritually advanced; they were educated and they respected the Earth and the universe. They were wise and understood the importance of living in accordance with universal law. They understood our divine DNA is a direct like to the Source. As organized religion started to spread across the lands, ancient practices were forced out of society. They were kept alive only by small sects of people, who practiced unnoticed.

Explore Your Sacred Truth

In recent years people have just begun to take the time to explore and understand what it means to live in spiritual consciousness. At one time it was thought that people in the West who lived spiritually were hippies or free spirits. They were referred to as nice people, but a little "out there." It is only in the last two decades or so that Western people have begun to adhere to alternative ways of worship. They are leaving behind conventional ways in search for a system that fits their spiritual and social lifestyles. People are learning that they have spiritual DNA and how to use it. As humans our auras are parallel to those of divine beings, making us omniscient like them. We also share other qualities. Not all humans were and are aware of this knowledge, but now it is available to you. So the true meaning of living in balance with your environment is keeping things in spiritual order.

Your biggest challenge will be to learn to use universal law in living both a human and a cosmic life. Spiritual beings trust in divine and universal forces to work within our system and guide us in how to help one another. You have no other alternative but to look at situations objectively. Human and spiritual life forces must nourish each other for the two energy sources to work in balance. When people do not find balance, they become consumed. You can't even the scales without balance. That is why everywhere you go people are looking for places to be heard and listened to!

Another trait we have as humans is we crave acceptance and want to be our true self! Spiritual beings give everyone the opportunity to be their own person and develop their abilities accordingly. This doesn't mean there is no discipline; it means everyone is willing to work together with one another in order to grow. Instead of seeking approval from others, we should

Surrounding Influences that Impact Our Spiritual Journey

learn from one another and co-exist together in acceptance and peace. Learn to make yourself happy and do things to nourish yourself; this is very important spiritually. When you are spiritually fed, you live in a healthy environment because the energy you release around you is positive. Whether it's your parents, children, friends, or partner, people will notice your frequency. This is very inspiring to them! People want to do better in all areas when they are surrounded by people who are balanced and encouraging of others in the way they act. There are seven billion people on the planet and we all share one thing in common: We all want to love and be loved. You are astounding in all you do. No other creatures on earth have as much depth as we do! You have the potential in you to do and become anything you want to be, don't ever forget it!

You are at the nexus of awareness. Once you achieve this level, your link with the divine changes into harmony with universal law. As you are learning and experiencing changes from within, let your mind extend into the universe. Try this exercise: Sit in a place that is peaceful. Sometimes I put on music and I close my eyes. I envision expanding my mind into the Oneness. After some time, I begin to allow my mind to travel. I am receptive to the deep vastness of the universe. Instead of thinking, I allow the transmissions of thought and visions to come to me. By allowing my mind to expand into oneness with the universe, my brain is connecting to the signals; in turn, I can receive the transmissions. Think of it as a form of communication. I want you to do the exercise just as I stated. Have paper and pen next to you so you can write down what happens to you. Look for the encoded message in what you write down.

Submerge yourself passionately in your spiritual lessons and ritual exercises. It is definitely an unequivocal experience, one that connects your mind to universal expansion. Are you aware that the most fulfilled and successful people follow this principle? Not only do they have perseverance, they have learned to be true spiritual beings. They have successfully navigated through life's obstacles, sometimes going through deep emotional trenches, and they have emerged victorious! You know why? Because they all share enormous belief in the power of faith. Their unconditional faith leads them to believe beyond the tangible. They choose to take a leap into the Divine. They call on everything that surrounds them and work it through the system "that all is possible within the Oneness." Allow yourself to become one with truth, and the only real truth is what you truly know is right. This is the essence that connects you with Source; it is your brain waves that help you to do it. Call it, if you will, the seeds of Creation manifesting in you!

As you allow this process to become part of your life, you'll notice how your being becomes centered. All that we've discussed is preparing you for a natural process that will take place as you grow. It is an ever-evolving transition. This is what takes you towards true enlightenment. It is a process that teaches you how to connect with higher sources and use them to evolve into a higher human. Your mind is learning to receive from all that is relevant and not from what is repetitive. You want to begin to see without any barriers. To excel you have to you have to use the power of Now. Let go of things that are past, don't hang on to them. If you do, you will always have unhealthy energy in your orb. I used the word orb because you have your own energy sphere. I speak throughout this book of a universal concept, which is the intricate web that interconnects all life. For many years this idea was rejected by Westerners, but it is now becoming widely accepted. This in itself demonstrates how your existence exists as multidimensional frequencies. This understanding brings a person deep satisfaction.

Keep in mind as your spiritual growth deepens that you can unlock the answers as to how universal laws work. There are no hidden doors once you begin to understand your true self and purpose. It really is simple: You live by a principle by which you develop the way you were meant to. Know and respect that you are entitled to this eminent gift of divine truth. Use it wisely. It is the only way for the natural power within divine law to work for you. It aides you to gather the knowledge you need to undertake a liberating psychic process. In doing so you are striving to reach enlightenment; that is why the process plays such an important role in your development. Do not be intimidated by these methods; they teach you how to grow. You want to come to a place where your spirit can flow freely. The beauty of this is it's such a natural process, and the feeling is so uplifting to your psychic well-being. You'll experience realizations about yourself that were hidden in your core, and your spiritual quest will become more focused. You are in the moment of total change, and it's now time to create order in your environment. By using your skills and your mind you will have the opportunity to increase your perception of things. This is how your mind receives wisdom.

STEPPING INTO ONENESS WITH NATURE AND THE SPIRITUAL WORLD

I'd like to introduce you to another aspect of the environment that plays a significant role in your development. It is called, Nature. Nature is in an integral part of our development and is at the center of oneness on earth. Nature is a natural resource in our environment, and it has been a guiding source for all forms of spirituality since antiquity. People in general have a natural appreciation for Nature. Just think of the last time you stopped and absorbed the natural beauty of a place. There are places on this planet where the sheer beauty overwhelms and encompasses you. Do you know there are electrical charges that manifest in all of Nature, including vegetation, soil, rocks, and the atmosphere, just to name a few? They are natural energy retainers and you can draw from them. Energy from natural elements can flow freely to you. It's is so phenomenal, what can happen within Nature's boundaries. Most people never realize that these elements have a layering of complex laws. They are independent movements of matter and energy. Just like meditation is an open doorway for humans to discover knowledge, Nature has the same effect. These principles are a science based on tangible results.

None of these practices require you to spend money to develop them. Once you comprehend the basic principles of each of these methods you can convert them into tools that will be of great service to you. When you want to do something with all your being, you commit to doing so. It is the same when you develop and awaken the real energies. Humans have been using Nature as a source since the Earth was first lived on. By learning how existence functions at every level of life you receive a direct transmission of wisdom and knowledge. Without realizing it you begin to put these principles to work for you. The ancient people worshiped freely within Nature and used the elements of the Earth. It enabled them to discover the essence of their being. They knew Nature was an element to use in unlocking oneness with other living things. They recognized the power that Nature holds, whether it was the trees, the sun or moon, plants, or the soil. They kept in balance with these elements and they knew that we have a relationship with them. To this day Nature gives us a sense of serenity and a nurturing balance. There is nothing as beautiful as watching a flower unfold and come to life.

Nature is a free gift and we should be mindful of doing our part to preserve and take care of it. Many artifacts were discovered throughout history proving Nature was used in connection with the Divine. There are stone circles, crop images, essential oils, crystals, herbs, and countless other elements from Nature that are still used today. The beauty of Nature is that it gives us its bounty to use.

Moving forward, things will begin to happen to you and, as your steps become bigger, you will grow tremendously in spirit. This is a time when confusion gives way to accomplishments and past mistakes are forgotten, freeing you to forge ahead. Keep in mind that destiny is powerful. Your bond with Nature undoubtedly plays a role in your journey. Learn to use Nature as another tool that helps you meet the true self. How does this happen? First, you have to begin to become one with Nature and see what influences it has on you. You will know what is beneficial to you as you seek and learn which element in Nature works for you. Sit and observe in silence and just listen. It's amazing what you'll see and discover. Once that happens, you will make the connection between relevancy and how the growth process evolves.

It is the same with the spiritual world and how it interconnects with the world we live in. A particular attitude starts to manifest in your current circumstances and a canvas unfolds making you see and think outside the box. You are starting to know your true inner self. You need to know this person who resides at your spiritual core. It is your true self that has what you need to nourish yourself from within. There are signals that are being transmitted to you. These signals are your own, designed for you. Use what you pick up as your personalized guide. Source and Spirit surround you. You are a divine spirit and you can connect through these methods. The guidance will be provided when you ask for it. You've heard it countless times from people who've also made the connection, they all say the same thing: Nature brought balance back to their lives; they finally came to understand the inter-connection Spirit and Nature have with one another. For many Nature is a portal to a secret realm, like a karmic pattern. That is why you'll hear people who have experienced it speak of Nature's underlying connection with Spirit. It allows you to see and understand the laws of Nature with clarity.

Interacting with Nature aligns our human and spiritual energies to interconnect in oneness. It is a complete merging of mind and spirit. It never ceases to amaze me, how this works. It teaches you how to reach illumination within yourself. The Source of the universe has provided for humankind, on both the physical and spiritual planes in order for us to become one with how the cycles work. The beginning of the inner work you will do is the shift into the Now. This system has been in place for a centuries. Gone are the old inhibitions that serve no purpose in your life. Your senses will vibrantly feel your emotions.

Meditation , visualization, and connecting with your inner self are friends of Nature. The three are core values of spiritual freedom. I would like you to try this exercise: Picture yourself in a garden. There are many different types of flowers in this garden. These flowers represent your life on earth. No two flowers are the same. The garden has many varieties, which represent the many opportunities available to you, but only one is a perfect fit for you. The parable is, each flower in the garden has a unique potential, just like you. Explore what is around you and, like the flowers in the garden, one will fit perfectly, with your name on it. Go discover your full potential and fulfill your life's purpose! Why else do you think you made the journey to this planet in the first place?

You are cultivating an attitude that comes from two planes, the spirit world and the physical world. When these two energies fuse together you will have a deeper understanding of what the human purpose is on Earth. Think of this pilgrimage as a journey to a distant land. View it as a road that you decided to walk, and along the way you enter a world of marvelous discovery, one that brings you revelations. Doubt is replaced with determination, and your daily progress leads you to learn who you are. It is such a deep level of spiritual understanding. Use the tools you were given to encompass the elements with an all-seeing eye. You are becoming ever-watchful; your senses are very powerful at this time.

Embracing the Energy

You are now in the Omnipresent! In order to experience the Omnipresent you must achieve a broad sense of mind expansion. The revelations that come to you from it are conditions and circumstances that influence your behavior; they allow you to see clearly on the internal and external levels. Planet Earth is ever-changing and so are its people. These principles are how you expand your attention to a state of awareness. Seeing beyond your ego is how true manifestation takes place. The rituals and tools are provided by the Divine, but you have to do the work to discover your true essence. Each of us is part of this vast universe. We each have a purpose and it is not impossible for us to understand our divine nature. Developing divine-like qualities is not only for a chosen few; it is for all of us! We were created as equals with our divine counterparts, only we chose to come to Earth temporarily and experience human life. We are meant to live in accordance with a purpose, one that evolves with the universe. Scientists are now acknowledging the interconnection between us and higher energy frequencies, which are no doubt divine energy sources. Whatever you do, don't let stereotypes condition your mind. Research and seek answers. This is a life-changing journey you are undertaking, and you should completely understand what it entails before taking it. Your thoughts are powerful and can help you shape your destiny.

As Dr. Wayne Dyer says : "If you change the way you look at things, the things you look at change." A very simple but true statement, which I interpret as looking through a lens that is different from the one you used to use. Your mind touches a truth that is way beyond the tangible and you are trusting that the spirit realm is working with you to aide and guide you on your journey. Dedication sometimes can be challenging, and still you will have to have it. The truth of universal law is simple, but you have to be dedicated to accessing your true self, the Source, and your guides. Ask them to clear any blockages that are keeping you from understanding your purpose. Don't worry, you will surmount anything that comes your way! You will have a positive outcome; this is only a transitional period.

A successful life is made by knowing how to find balance and do what is good for you. It's your personal takeoff to your spiritual destination; it is your blueprint all mapped out for you that comes from a transcendent Source of energy that is everpowerful. Throughout the centuries, many have gone seeking for this knowledge. The impressive part is that we all have divine knowledge encoded in us. It is the beings who instinctively

Surrounding Influences that Impact Our Spiritual Journey

know this who are champions at accessing it. Think of all this as a fine piece of fabric where all the threads are woven together perfectly. The teaching is to learn how to connect your soul to the Supreme soul. Through your subconscious mind you establish a relationship between the Supreme and your soul. The knowledge you acquire brings with it a penetrating understanding of life. You may ask, how is this going to come about? It comes from unlocking the scripted code within you. Now some of you may raise the issue that this sounds controversial, but it is not. This is a piece of ancient wisdom, and you only have to practice it yourself to reach the final answer on your own. I expect each of you to question. If you don't, how will you discover the truth?

Although every human is born with psychic abilities, not everyone is willing to develop them. Rebirthing is a process; it is not handed to you, you have to bring it forth. The connection that is taking place between you and the divine realm is real. In the beginning you might feel a change in your body; don't be alarmed, it is normal and it will pass. You are purging yourself of old toxins. This means you are getting ready to go to the next level. You are at the turning point. Now is the time to stay focused. The blessings are coming! You will see that each person in your life has a connection, and those that don't will go their separate ways. The eclipse that was overshadowing you is dissipating, being replaced by new karma. Each one of us has a journey that leads us to our destination. There could be one or many journeys that we make depending on how many other lives we've led. Each one is unique. Don't worry how the union happens between you and the Supreme Soul. Once you are receptive it all will begin to flow. Spiritual enlightenment is about being in the present, the Now.

Once you experience the energy connection, you can open yourself to a colossal amount of information. I suggest you pay attention to everything that is around you at this time because where others see nothing, you will see the encoded messages. I will continue to write these words throughout the book: You are born with a divine birthright, but you have to participate in the exercises in order to fulfill it. In other words, you have the choice to bring it forth or keep it dormant. The first step is to love yourself because you are a divine soul; the next is to be kind to yourself. When you are in harmony with yourself, everything else is easier to do because you have confidence. When you respect yourself first you can operate from love. You may ask, what will I get out of this? For one, you will be grounded and clear. Understand that peace, humility, kindness, compassion, and empathy will replace anger, greed, sorrow, regret, and ego. It's a nice trade-off, don't you agree?

The time has come when you will set aside what others think of your spiritual choices and do the things that make you who you are. In the same way other people live by their philosophies, you should live by yours. One of the first things I tell people is that the key to being completely whole is to discover who your true self is! Why? you ask. Because for the first time you are peeling back the layers that were covering you. Makes a lot of sense, doesn't it? You are experiencing the universal flow of energy. This is the blessing of nourishing yourself from within; miraculously the solutions that are needed come with less effort. You are different from most people who will blossom and fade in a predictable lifestyle. The path you are taking now is a process of change and renewal. Think of it as a "river that flows freely." This current takes you through many changes, but you are closer to your arrival than you think. You are stepping into what I call "a pure energy field." My goal is to help you understand how your practices work in your spiritual and daily life.

Surrounding Influences that Impact Our Spiritual Journey

I call this "stepping into pure energy." When I speak in these terms, I am giving you a way to visualize the magnitude of what is taking place in you. I do this because I want you to understand how our divine DNA works for us. The goal is to help you use it effectively, so that its positives effects improve your life. I guide you to use the elements surrounding you because they have benefits for you. Humans are wired to have a thirst for spirituality. This is part of our consciousness. Why do you think we always lean towards a higher source to show us an easier way? When you are a true practitioner of higher truth, you experience a rejuvenation of mind and spirit. You hold an impressive and amazing strength inside you. By becoming aware of it and learning how to use it, you unlock the answers to the questions you have. These writings share elements that are necessary for your spiritual growth. Every spiritual tradition speaks of how basic elements make up what we are. The ancients taught and lived according to Nature. They knew everyone and everything is connected and affected by their surroundings.. There is a conscious evolution taking place in you which is affected by your surroundings. I have named it a transitory world that impacts all living bodies, their senses, and their life force.

The Earth is like a womb; it gives birth to all life on the planet. Everything that lives is dependent upon it! So ask yourself, why would I not want help from this powerful energy source? This is why I am constantly encouraging you to connect with your inner self. Remember, I told you, we all are going towards the same Source, but each of us has our own unique blueprint of how to do it. This is the central component of these principles and teachings. You are taking action to incorporate these principles in your life. The easiest way to begin is to start with the exercises in the beginning chapters. They are easy to understand and become effortless with practice. Knowledge will be transmitted to you through meditation and by surrendering to the divinity that is in you. The process of complete human development is taking place in you. As you complete each step you will have a better understanding of how existence functions. The energies that you are using are very real and tangible. You have guides that will move things along. Now would be a good time to start welcoming them into your life.

Combined with what you are learning, you have to have trust and faith. Universal law works within its own structure. Things begin to happen at their destined time, and sometimes they happen in the most unpredictable way. The trust and faith you have draw energy to you, even when you think they are not. This is the practical way to evolve spiritually. This is your realization, revelation, and discovery of the true self. You are freeing yourself from the constraints of self-doubt and ignorance. Don't hesitate to use visualization in order to make changes. By visualizing you're helping to make the images you see a reality. Nature provides other elements for you to use to connect the energy of the images to yours. These practices were used by people for centuries. They work, and they are coming back to be used by many. This is the reason it is called a major turning point in a person's life. You are completely transforming. You will know how to use spiritual teachings and the elements to gain overall balance. Don't waste your newfound knowledge on infertile pursuits; use it to commune with the Divine.

Everyone on this planet has an inner voice; the problem is people ignore it. I am telling you to take the time to listen for it; it will guide you on a visible spiritual path. I read this phrase: "Each day the night births to a sunrise, the haze giving way to what is to come." Think about the dimensions to the statement.

Surrounding Influences that Impact Our Spiritual Journey

It can apply to you, too, because with each day you can venture into activities that allow you to understand the universe is God's. It is a philosophy that can be summarized this way: You are a being that ventured out to discover your connection with Source and the universe, and what you uncovered led you to positive life-changing experience. Keep expanding the energetic connections with your surroundings and tap into the divine realm. It is your birthright. Use it and become fulfilled! You can begin to call upon the surrounding environment to help you implement your life's purpose.

VI

The Power of Communicating Divinely

STARTING THE DIVINE CONNECTION

DREAMS, MEDITATION, TRANCELIKE states, talking to angels, telepathic communication all help you speak to the Divine. These are portals to communicating with Spirit. The portals are not the same for everyone. However, the communication starts by your opening your being to divine energy. It is a world filled with intrigue and mystery that directly links you to Spirit, a world that recently has begun to be more openly discussed. For the open-minded, it brings new possibilities of expanding the conscious and subconscious mind and developing the ability to communicate with divine energy beings. Just think, the universe is prepared to send countless messengers to you in various forms of divine being.

There are people that are apprehensive about believing that humans have the ability to speak with Spirit. This relates to how humans have been conditioned to think. We separated ourselves from Spirit in our minds. Our minds were conditioned—notice I said were—to believe we are less than divine beings . Which is not true! Our spirits live in our bodies and make it possible to communicate with divine beings. Speaking with them is not just for a select few; each of us has the capability to do it. Our energy

The Power of Communicating Divinely

frequencies can reach the same wavelengths as spirit energy. The differences between spirits and us is they are nonphysical beings and we are not. Not everyone wants to develop the skill to speak divinely, and that is why some see it as taboo. I believe it is fair to say appearances are not always what they are perceived to be. And as you discover the true essence of communicating divinely, you can use it for your benefit. I refer to it as "developing your own sensory receptors." When your receptors are in tune with the universe, it's as if you glide into making intelligent decisions. You are a on a totally different wavelength.

This development is linked to the nature of science through the subconscious. The statement may seem a little dense, so let me explain it to you as it was taught to me: Science is the study of things in the universe that are beyond our reach. In order for our subconscious to expand with the universe, the mind and Nature must become parallel. You are going to learn how to visualize your mind in an ever-expanding state, just like that of the universe. When you are in this state, the first thing your spirit will feel is light. Then you know your body and spirit have merged with the vastness, and your entire being is open to communicate. There are a number of ways that people do it; the one that is right for you will be made known to you. This is a good time to pay attention to images and dreams, and when your inner voice speaks, listen. In the beginning you will have to rely mainly on your intuition and senses. As a student there will be times when you are learning in ways you didn't think possible.

The best advice I can give you is to let your intelligence lead the way. Ask questions, do the ritual exercises, and take in new knowledge in order to make a logical determination for yourself. Think about the magnitude of the statement I am about to make: The majority of people on this planet pray according to their culture and faith. They pray as if it is second nature to them. Ask them if they can communicate with the Divine. Most of them would say no! Praying is a form of exchange with nonphysical beings. Most people aren't conscious that when they pray they are communicating on another dimensional level. There are thousands of people who can attest to speaking and receiving messages from spirit beings. The ancients recorded their rituals and interactions in order for us to learn the techniques they used. They knew humans are connected to sources of energy that come from universal dimensions.

People who are open to a higher level of consciousness realize the principle of cause and effect in spiritual enlightenment when it is practiced correctly. Practicing communicating with the Divine not only brings spiritual fulfillment; it has other benefits! Ask anyone who communicates in this way and they all say the same thing. They rely on the vibrations they receive and follow their guidance. They say it is always the wisest option. To put it simply, communicating with higher beings is a source of nurturing. Being open-minded to fundamental laws helps you act with intelligence. I like to equate the experience to this statement: The lotus floats silently on the water taking in Creation, making its way on the river, as it stands in its own beauty. That is who you are. A person standing at one with Creation.

Expansion has it benefits. You see a truth and a beauty that was previously hidden from you. Before we go further I would like to explain: It is not true that in order to communicate with the Divine you have to hear voices. That's an old wives' tale! There are people who hear spirits; but the fact is there are many ways to receive transmissions. In order to do it you must be open spiritually for the exchange to happen and the portal to open. What prevents the majority of people from gaining access to the spirit world is they think it can't be done. They think connecting spiritually and receiving messages from divine realms is taboo, and so they mentally block it. Use the tools you've learned along with the ritual exercises and see what happens over the next few months. It is an essential requirement in order for you to receive the transmissions. One of the things I would like you to remember when you begin to communicate is that it is a remarkably elastic feeling that stretches you deep within your core. Words will begin to come through as the pathway to your subconscious is opening. This is the time to listen carefully because you may get flooded with messages.

In the beginning you might feel little emotional shifts occurring within you. It is normal and temporary. One of the things I would like you to start practicing is becoming friends with the silence. Stillness heightens your awareness. In the silence you can hear clearly what your inner self is saying. As you cross parallel worlds you will feel and act according to higher wisdom. Ancient traditions practiced this for centuries, all against a backdrop of established rituals in a belief system that is now resurfacing. Despite centuries of attacks from religious leaders to control the way people developed spiritually, people are making the effort to communicate and listen to a higher calling, one that is guiding them to live a more balanced and fulfilling life.

In today's modern society it is becoming more widespread and people are leaving behind traditions that no longer full their spiritual growth. This was written by Tonya Ann Arnold : "You are the seed, and God is the manifestation. You are the seed and God is the actuality. You are the potential, God is the actual. God is your destiny and you are carrying your destiny for many without looking at it, because your eyes are fixed somewhere in the future. They don't look at the present. Here and now, everything is as it should be, if you are ready to look." This sums it up: When you are ready to see, it is waiting for you! What? you may ask. You spiritual blueprint is waiting for you! And it's time to put it to use!

We each have our own blueprint. It's unique and tailor-made to fit us. When we use it in the correct way, we are capable of achieving far beyond what we can perceive. There is a lot of information available that enables us to decipher how to make it work for each of us. Learning how to enter into a trancelike state gives you the opportunity to merge your thoughts with higher beings. After-all, we are the descendants of Divine Essence. It is a co-evolution in which our biogenetics are finely attuned to divine sources. The ability for this is in your brain. Not only are you communicating divinely; you have a guiding force with you.

I would like you to do this simple exercise: You'll need a pen and paper and a quiet place. You may play music and light incense if it relaxes you. I'd like you to sit in a comfortable position. Begin to take deep breaths. Slowly and deeply begin to inhale and exhale. As you relax, you'll begin to feel at one with your breathing. Now, I would like you to call on your spirit guide and ask your guide to step into your energy. Wait until you feel your guide is with you. You'll know. Either you'll feel their presence, or you will have a knowing feeling; you will feel the shift when it happens. Now ask a question. Ask a simple question; for example: My spirit guide, can you to show me how to connect with my higher self? Stay in this place as long as you need to, and when you are ready, open your eyes and come back to the present. Write down everything that comes to you. Jot down words, pictures, smells, colors—all that flashes to you. When you are finished, thank your guides. Read what you wrote. You

The Power of Communicating Divinely

will be surprised at the encoded messages you'll receive. I want you to be aware that for some it might take a few sessions of practice; don't get discouraged, keep going. For others it will happen immediately. The energy that passes through you is amazing. Mindboggling messages come to you. We once did this exercise in a group I created. An amazing spiritual sister and teacher led the exercise. I participated as part of the group. The messages I received were exactly correct! As you progress you will receive more guided messages and become accustomed to channeling communication from the Divine. You can ask your guides their names or make spiritual contact with an ascended master. These spirit beings were folks like Jesus when they lived on Earth. They were and are teachers of humanity. All these experiences are enhancing your development. Your brain waves develop an intricate thinking process, leading you to make significant changes in your existence.

In antiquity, it was common practice to communicate with and rely on the subconscious to help expand the mind, strengthen discipline, and further psychological and spiritual development. In modern times, there is a surge of people who recognize the need to become spiritually one with Creation. The very same principles you are learning have been taught to humanity for centuries. They are systematic universal laws describing what is called the independent movement of matter and energy. Imagine waking your consciousness to all the possibilities available to your human form. Meditation is one of the most important exercises you can use to help you. The practice frees your mind from the bonds of attachment. I mentioned earlier that most people think they are closed off to divine communication. The truth is you are always receiving transmissions; you just don't open your mind to them. Every time you hear that small voice say something, it is intuition calling you. That is divine communication. Divine communication is your birthright, everyone can access it. I'll say it to you again and again: The key to receiving the transmissions is to be open to them. Your mind has to expand into your subconscious where there is no ego to censor your thoughts.

It all comes from expanding your mind and, of course, commitment on your part. We often refer to our five outer senses. So how do you think you discover your sixth sense, the sense that is invisible to your physical self, the one that is always with you but you fail to recognize, your lifelong roommate. Remember, I said you have to learn stillness. You have to be in a peaceful frame of mind. That's how your mind filters messages to you. From this moment you are entering into the secret of your existence. The communication will be between you and higher energies. You will hear things that are only meant for you, about your journey and what path is right for you to take. Suddenly the communication is distinct and you are exposed to a higher reason, one that will enhance your thought process. Don't be fooled; there are divine helpers that are waiting to guide you. Learning how to communicate in a unique and personal way gives you access to a higher intelligence. And through your newfound discoveries, you are creating the empowerment necessary to sustain your life force. Look for the subtle signs. They come in many ways. A soft message, a mental image, your inner self fluttering softly in your ear. Higher reason wants to communicate with you! Your guides will receive your frequency. That lets them know you are open to and ready for the communication. In order for you to begin the exploration of mind expansion and its connection with higher life sources you will have to begin somewhere. This book is an excellent reference to get you started. The exercises are easy to understand and simple to do. Each is significant and they all interact with each other to bring you a step further in your spiritual development. They are natural to universal law and the power of being in the Now.

Taking this path leads you to develop to your highest potential, revealing to you a new perspective in seeing and doing things. Each of us has to have confidence; it is essential in our life. If we don't have it, we find it hard to shed our shell and expand. Spiritual fulfillment keeps us well-rounded and steady. It helps build courage within us. That is what we want, a system that fits into our life, one that we can implement at our own pace. We want to free our minds of the impurities that block our senses. Whether you are aware of it or not, our entire existence revolves around finding the meaning of our life. We instinctively know that we have a higher purpose and we seek it. The human is an insightful and creative species. I am guiding you towards this type of communication for you to become tuned in to your true spiritual essence.

There are many spiritual guides who can help you. Pick one whose energy you can feel. Every guide that is true to the teachings of universal law will tell you so. You have to learn how to remove the clutter from your mind. This is why I teach you how to use techniques to quiet the mind. It is so crucial and at times so hard to do. Your perseverance is essential when the intangible is present. I lived this reality. I am guiding you and teaching you simple methods to use. I understand the emotions that you will experience on your spiritual path. Go back to the basics whenever you need to. Meditate and breathe. It balances your energy and helps you to think clearly. This is why the term "become unattached" is used.

Think of the mind and universe as a blank canvas. Let the pictures come to you. A drawing tells a story. The divine realm does the same thing. Metaphorically, your being and the Divine are merging with your subconscious. We're aiming for the subconscious to be in the state of manifestation, where higher intelligence can coexist and interact with us. This is the stage where the subconscious is relaxed and your being is in an insightful state. Being unattached is the first activity you have to learn. It teaches you to stop your mind from being caught up with conscious thought. The next level is to become quiet. Now you're taking the veil off, allowing more thoughts to process through you—images, messages, visions, etc. You are ready to drift into unconscious thought and into the realm of Spirit with no attachments. The progression unfolds seamlessly. The ultimate goal is mind expansion. This is how your conscious mind opens up. This is the process you follow. You have to practice the exercises. Remember, you are clearing out the clutter, so have patience in the beginning.

If you understand that you are able to receive astral frequencies and that spiritual energy is being transmitted to you, understanding the seed of manifestation shouldn't be difficult. As you receive these energies you are going to project visual images and connect them with the energies. As your mind expands into the Oneness, it receives higher frequencies that pulse through your body. They are called charges of energy. This is the point of pinnacle manifestation. As you visualize, all the elements you are drawing from are merging together. This is called the conscious or awakened state. You have expanded into the Oneness. Your whole being is acting like a conduit, pulling all the energy towards you. You are now being connected to higher wavelengths and self-transformation is occurring. Your whole being is being revitalized. You are a higher being.

As you reconnect with your divine DNA and you pick up the communications, your perspective on things become very clear. You intelligently see that there are many ways that spiritual growth happens. It is not limited, but very varied.

The Power of Communicating Divinely

Your mind is developing at a fast pace. It is the central root that comprehends hidden knowledge. I call it the "receptive power to communicate." Picture it as a universal transmitter. You are penetrating the nonphysical and connecting the human soul to mental phenomena. You are becoming sensitive to the supernatural influences on your spiritual nature.

It is not prohibited to practice sacred teachings. In our modern world, scientists are now researching and acknowledging that the mind has a subconscious that is separate from the body. The ancients said this for centuries. With all the information that is available, I want you to come to the logical conclusion for yourself. Your intuition will lead you to your truth. The people you meet who live this way will tell you simply that spirituality is based on each person's experience of the truth, and the road leading to it is practice. In order to understand, you must experience it. There's nothing taboo about it at all. We practice and experience so we may rely on proven qualities that can help us to grow. As the masters of Confucianism say, "You will transmit what is taught to you without making up anything."

There are a number of reasons to believe that sacred teaching and ancient civilizations all learned spiritual principle from Source Energy, which rooted its knowledge in the people on Earth. Modern society with all it technologies still cannot understand how the Egyptians built the pyramids, or how the Mayans built their intricate temples. These civilizations had the knowledge of the mystical sciences. They were advanced civilizations and they communicated with higher beings. When you think about it, it is the only logical explanation. All the evidence supporting it is logical. With all our modern-day advancements, the greatest of minds on the planet still cannot figure out how these marvels were constructed!

Explore Your Sacred Truth

Communicating with higher beings is essential for understanding. Practicing makes it a reality. It always amazes me how people can believe in the sublime but not in the higher sciences.

It is fair to say that in order to have spiritual insight, you must see yourself first. In order to see yourself, you have to remove the veil. To remove it, you must work to change what you don't like. We all wish for things to come easily, but in truth we must work for what we want. Your strength will be tested at times. This is all part of it. You have to live in accord with spiritual principles. That is the only way to discover hidden knowledge. Guidance from higher sources also helps the growth of understanding; but the decision to develop it comes from you, and you have to be serious in wanting to find it.

One of the biggest misconceptions people have about ancient traditions is they think they are complex systems. When they are broken down into easy-to-understand instructions, they aren't intimidating. People then realize that their goals can be achieved. These traditions help us advance toward subconscious freedom. Each person has the advantage of being skillful. To be in a peaceful state spiritually takes away so much useless baggage. It allows you to look at what needs to be changed in your life. The courage rises in you and you do it! You learn who the true you is, the very essence of who you are uncensored. We are all connected on the planet. These are the basics for understanding the principle of cause and effect in communicating with the Divine.

The Role of Angels

No discussion of communicating with the Divine would be complete if we didn't include angels. According to what is written, angels existed even before humans. They are the messengers of Source Energy and are called "spirits of the light." Every

The Power of Communicating Divinely

person on Earth has been touched by an angel. They are always in the background. Many extraordinary accounts have been told by people about how angels interceded on their behalf. Their mission ranges from warning us of danger to helping us according to our needs. They also act as guiding forces that give us renewed spiritual clarity. Communication with them is widespread. They have been interacting on Earth since its inception.

A study was conducted in Great Britain in 2002 in which 350 people who said they had had encounters with angels were interviewed . They described their experiences in various ways. Some had visions and touching, others smelled fragrances, many were pushed out of danger's way. Still others saw angels appear in the form of extraordinary beings. Angels are capable of great feats. Communicating with them has been recorded throughout the centuries. Legend says that when you are born an angel touches your lips so you will remain silent about what you already know, and so you do not remember anything about the higher dimension you come from.

There are angels who are assigned to Earth to help us with our earthly mission. In the studies conducted, the people who had actual interactions with Angels say they changed their lives completely. Some even say they felt a change in their energy field. These spirit beings are pure energy. Your complete acceptance of them leads them straight into your life. This leads to divine communication without boundaries. There are angels who work with the elements: fire, earth, air, and water. Their tasks differ from each other. When people communicate with them they may be asking for help such as purification, balance, positive transformation, harmony, or protection, things of that sort. In short, angels have the task of keeping humans balanced.

Explore Your Sacred Truth

It is said that angels can pass through our lives and we don't recognize them. This means that they are ever-present and sometimes work in the background. Their energy flow comes from the Divine, making them very powerful. Angels are everywhere and they act as intermediaries on our behalf. If this is new for some of you, I would like you meditate and let your mind expand on the subject. Use your intelligence to guide you in your understanding. We have gone to the moon, engineered telescopes that see millions of light years away; yet when it come to the nonphysical we hesitate. If you say to me, how could this be possible? I would reply, how could it not? Whether we acknowledge it or not, we are souls who are made up of energy. We can communicate we higher beings! Angels are waiting for you to send them an invitation.

One angel who needs no invitation and has been with you since birth is your guardian angel. That is your personal representative on Earth. This angel has a deep understanding of you. There have been accounts where people have said they spoke to their guardian angel, who acted as teachers to them. Belief is widespread in all religions about angels, and that each human being at birth is assigned a personal one directly from Source. These divine beings not only communicate with us through our dreams and soft callings to our subconscious; they protect us from unforeseeable circumstances. They are with us till our departure.

People have different experiences when communicating with higher beings. Communication comes in varied ways. We covered the fundamentals, suggesting how to begin this communication within your own psychic framework. Whether you are getting messages directly, or through images, or by speaking to angels—even if you are communicating telepathically—you're doing it.

The Power of Communicating Divinely

It is real and it has been done for centuries. There are many books available for reading on the subject. There are gifted beings who teach these principles. They experience first-hand the frustration and elation that they encountered on their path. There are many ways to learn and grow when you want to further develop mind expansion and the ability to communicate on higher-dimensional levels. We are all striving to evolve our minds with in oneness with Creation.

This is your spiritual journey, one that will bring many revelations to you. The experiences are your own. You are in the driver's seat to spiritual enlightenment. There might be a few twists and turns to contend with. So what! As you continue to grow, you are evolving into higher intelligence. I am guiding you in the understanding that you have been selected to participate in evolving into your highest self on Earth. If you are reading this book, the Divine has directed you to do so. It is up to you to surpass yourself to accomplish something extraordinary. Keep growing and practicing. Soon you'll routinely be communicating with the Divine.

VII

Dimensional Energies and Your Spirit

EXPANDING THE MIND

THINK ABOUT THIS statement: "There is no beginning and no end in the universe!" For a moment let's expand our minds to consider, "Your spirit is part of the universal system," one in which massive energies are living and expanding into other dimensions. Just as Source is incarnated in you, the invisible world has energetic portals and domains that effect you. Your spirit links to these energies and then you can tap into them. As your spiritual intellect is shifting, you'll be arriving at another threshold and turning point in your spirituality.

The spiritual journey on Earth is about change and growth. We first learn to accept and then we can let go. And as we progress, we learn how to evolve into higher beings. This is part of the journey I have named ,"incarnating your spirit into dimensional energies." As your mind expands, your subconscious travels and you learn how to receive energies that come from far-off galaxies. This is why we do the exercises and direct ourselves to awareness, because we want to continually reach new insight in our development. You are expanding your mind in order to gain insight deep within your soul. This is called separating from the illusion that is created in your waking state and learning how to develop the subconscious.

Dimensional Energies and Your Spirit

Expect things to change as you progress. Your observation skills will become remarkable and as you reach new physic levels their counterparts will merge together and form an interior light in you. I refer to it as a fusion where energies meet and expand into higher dimensional spheres. Visions or flashings come into your subconscious rather quickly when this happens. As these waves move through you, a guiding source of energy shows you the workings of cause and effect in reality.

The whole spiritual journey is extremely valuable; even the challenges serve a purpose. It is a living stream in which your true self and the Divinity unite. You're letting your subconscious mind go to different spiritual dimensions, to where you can encounter the larger, expanded version of you.

Give your attention to your spiritual energy first. Our everyday life is connected to it. As you are changing and experiencing these newfound revelations, the obstacles that seemed to block you become manageable. You are training the unconscious to receive vibrations that help to empower you as a higher being. This is the reason we practice. Developing your unconscious depends on your willingness to wake up the Divine in you. Once you say yes, everything starts to unfold according to your blueprint. When you surrender to higher reason, you're encouraging a positive transformation to happen. Suddenly you realize the importance of Oneness and Creation. And each dimension serves a different purpose. Your instincts will become your greatest strength. You will rely on your intuition to guide you as you discover the meaning behind each event.

Many people work with energy long-distance. They heal, send out energy waves, communicate, and do spiritual channeling. Expanding the subconscious through different dimensional portals is nothing that hasn't been done before, and you can do it too!

Explore Your Sacred Truth

The good knowledge you acquire will help you demonstrate greater flexibility in growing your consciousness to new dimensional levels. Mind expansion teaches you how to step into things. When you are connected with higher energies your thoughts become elastic, your thinking process becomes flexible and so much more useful than if your mind is conditioned to only one way of thinking. All of us have experienced having to step into issues. When that happens it can leave us feeling vulnerable. However, there are elements in Nature that allow us to complete each level of growth and then go on to the next. I suggest writing at intervals about your journey. As you write, your blueprint is unfolding before you. A journal is good to keep handy. It serves as a great reference point.

Each of us is on our own spiritual journey. This path is one of intelligence, one on which you can demonstrate your human side and awareness. Each person on the journey will have a different experience doing so. Be comfortable in knowing that you are free to develop your spiritual life at your own pace. As you ascend, you gain wisdom by dominating your thoughts. Your inner voice guides you well now and your intuition is growing stronger. You are the master of what you want to gain from this journey. The philosophy of the teachings is simple. The path you are on is leading you to be in oneness with Source and Creation.

There is a worldwide epidemic that I refer to as the never-ending race. This mindset disconnects us from our spirituality. But there is a movement arising among people to change it. Spiritual beings say slow down. Learn to connect with positive energies to discover you true self. Spirituality teaches us to be intelligently open-minded. By doing so, a perspective comes to you as you join your energy with energies from other dimensions. It's an opening to new vistas and developments.

Dimensional Energies and Your Spirit

We become centered in the physical, emotional, mental, and spiritual aspects ourselves. Using these techniques is a way to enrich your daily and spiritual life. Some accustomed to more traditional ways may find it hard to believe or accept. As in anything else you do, base your understanding on the results and your experience. When you understand clearly, you can make the right choices. These teachings are to free your mind.

The first time I made the connection with Spirit it was brief but intense. I felt energy from within traveling to another plane. I instinctively knew I was connecting with higher energy. I felt a spirit-to-Spirit connection. The fusion was telepathic in nature, and as I let go, the messages were precise. My mind was elastic, and I could feel Creation as it was unfolding. It was a major turning point in my development. Each time my experience is a little different, and some days I don't make the connection I want. I don't worry because I know it is all part of the paradox. I am sharing my experience with you so you get a sense of some of the things that can happen as you attempt to merge with higher ,levels. Understand it is a process that happens. Don't think something is wrong just because it's an off day.

I would like you to try this guided exercise: For this you will use meditation and detachment to reach your objective. Keep pen and paper handy. You're going to begin by using the breathing techniques you've learned from the previous meditation exercises. What we are going to practice is how to merge your energy with higher-dimensional energy. Start by finding a calm and undisturbed place. When you are ready, I would like you to breathe until your mind resets into calmness. You'll notice the calmer you get, the lighter your body feels. As you enter into the calm state, I would like you to surrender to detachment. Try this by letting your mind drift into oneness with the stillness. The best way is to just free-flow into it and let it carry you. As you let go, the frequencies of the energies connect. You may feel some slight trepidation as the two energies merge. This is the point of union between mind and Creation. When this occurs things can happen quickly and vividly. Knowledge is being passed on in a collective way and is being retained in your mind.

In my first encounter with the Divine, I felt Creation being born in an extraordinary sense. I was able to see a picture of events unfolding in my subconscious. This allowed me to receive a series of revelations that helped me to see clearly what my purpose was here on Earth. The feeling was very distinct. It turned out to be an extremely significant experience for me. That is why I say keep pen and paper handy. It is a way of keeping yourself focused on the true experience. Remember, all of your energetic forces are engaging in psychic activity. You are entering into the awakening of the subconscious. Even the simple things that happen on the spiritual path have a divine purpose. My suggestion to you is to look at these activities as a puzzle. The pieces are there for you to put together and you're being accompanied by divine guidance as you do it. These forces are there to help you move onward, especially at the time of ascension. The will of your spirit is merging with the will of the Divine. Powerful change is happening to you on the subconscious level and spiritual forces are helping you to see with clarity. Embrace these moments.

You Are a Supreme Being

The human element was designed to have superior spiritual knowledge. This is why people begin to practice the rituals consistently, because they want to develop spiritually. Who doesn't want knowledge, especially of spiritual matters? Our divine blueprint connects with the process, and simultaneously we learn to adjust to different dimensional atmospheres as we physically remain in the material world. Our life is an extension of Source energy and higher spiritual life forces. We are shifting from the material world as we know it to the spiritual world where our energies are stripped of ego. Pay attention and listen to the messages you are receiving. The time has arrived where your energy is well spent and where you can evolve and gain access to higher consciousness. Matter is subject to natural law just as we need air to breathe. As a global community we developed different ways to worship, when in truth natural laws work the same way for everyone. One has to practice in order to determine how they make sense to you.

Energy is in motion and it lives. Whether you realize it or not, you access different energies in your everyday life. You experience this as using your will power or as a shift in energy. Everything has energy on this planet! On the spiritual journey we want to transform these energies into positive reinforcements of our daily life process. We want to have balance between our spiritual beliefs and social environment. We strive towards living to our fullest potential instead of merely existing. Our mind expands into the vastness of the universe. We can develop according to our blueprint. As with anything else you do, be conscious of the choices you make. As you focus on natural law, expect things to happen that allow you to see cause and effect. Nothing about this is fixed. The experiences that people have are different but real. This is how we learn from one another. We begin to understand the parallels that universal or divine law create in our life on Earth. The experience changes you to a better you.

Explore Your Sacred Truth

There are laws that govern the universe. Through advanced technology scientists are recording the evolutionary process of the universe. It's ever-expanding as Creation unfolds and sustains itself. This represents only a speck of the data uncovered. Scientists say much more is yet to be discovered. Look at our planet as it lives and sustains itself. So why isn't it possible to access our divine DNA? This is why you'll always hear spiritual people tell you to make friends with stillness. It is propitious for understanding how things work. You have the power of illumination in you but you haven't used it yet. Now is the time to see if there is anything that is preventing you from being spiritually open. If there is, you'll have to learn how to free your mind from unrealistic beliefs that hinder you. This is the opportunity for you to gain access to your higher consciousness. Your whole being has to be open to connect mind and spirit to other energy sources.

Everything in this book guides you gently into the practices you'll need on your journey. As you continue forward and complete one cycle, a new one begins. In my studies and experiences, I learned that each individual should start with what feels right for them. So many times people misunderstand this and they become frustrated. They become overwhelmed or think something is wrong. I understand it all! That is why I'm taking a much more relaxed approach in guiding you. More people than not experience these things. You are not alone. I suggest when you begin to connect with higher sources, start at a pace that feels right for you. As you become more integrated with the process your being is led towards purity, honesty, and revelation. You reach higher astral levels where the frequencies will irrefutably increase your potential. Don't resist the change. Go with it because change in itself is normal.

Dimensional Energies and Your Spirit

Mind expansion begins with change. Take a look at Nature; it is always growing or dying. Same with mind expansion. Either you allow it to grow or you never use it and it ceases to exist. That said, manifestation begins at different rates of vibration. You accelerate the change at the rate you choose. Doing so allows you to develop naturally and continually improve. The beauty of it all is you are creating your journey at a pace at which you can embrace the changes necessary to align you with the laws of the universe. You can connect with energies that already hold the reality of how you want to live on Earth. Discovering this power within you is another step in working with your divine birthright. It takes place at a higher level of consciousness and increases awareness. It's a process of inner power and spiritual enlightenment. You understand that everything has a purpose and you will come to know that the messages you receive are intended to give you answers to your underlying questions.

A new perspective on daily life processes is evolving to benefit you. You're not merely a follower of beliefs; you embody them. The will of Spirit is uniting with your consciousness, leading you to know yourself better, both consciously and subconsciously. Your mind will enrich itself to contain a resplendent balanced energy. Think about what you want to create as you call on your subconscious. This is a shift of great intellectual freedom and newly acquired knowledge. It's a complete awakening of your mind and a deep connection to your soul. The elements you are using in this process are raising the vibrations around you. Your natural divinity is helping you to evolve into your higher self. This path teaches you courage, humanism, and determination.

You are in the midst of a spiritual evolution. By looking deeply within yourself you will see the core of your being, empowering yourself to generate positive energies around you. Everything that is happening contributes to your spiritual awakening and is of benefit in your current affairs. You shift from a state that was passive into one that is sustained and fulfilled divinely. Numerous sources document the process of connecting to higher energy frequencies, recording stories of the interactions of humans with higher beings. These have existed from the beginning of Creation.

Mankind is moving towards a shift. Everything as we know it on Earth is changing. So many are seeking spiritual liberty, it's creating spontaneous change. Thanks to this way of thinking, people seeking inner enlightenment are creating a new space in which they can make higher communications happen. They are discovering new mental strengths and learning to dominate old habits that once conditioned their minds.

Now you know how to make the connection with the universe through natural elements. This chapter is all about feeling the flow of energy and tapping into your divine subconscious. Here your inner self is encouraging you to move forward to where manifestation can take place. The divine flow you are creating keeps you focused and aligned with Source energy. Now is a good time to stay grounded by doing the rituals you've learned. Meditation can be exceptionally helpful in connecting with astral realms.

Raising your own frequencies by contact with higher sources enhances your sensory perception. Your awakened conscious state becomes aware of the energy of other dimensional , giving you the capacity to adapt with flexibility and become autonomous in approaching the events of your life. The connection is not static; it's flowing and creative. Your mind is free to absorb all you are learning. The spiritual experiences you are having add significant growth and new encounters to your life. Awakening to your true self is awakening to the divine realm in you. What I am saying to you is get to know your divine identity. As it lives in you, it directly connects you to the divine world. The key to awakening in all spiritual knowledge is to know the true self. Once you know who you are, a barrier to higher consciousness is overcome. You are able to access different astral regions at will.

You have the opportunity to restore the divine nature that is you. Each person has different experiences. Their story is different. That is the beauty of the spiritual path. Mystical in nature, it consists entirely of divine essence and comes in various intellectual forms. Truly, that is how divinity expands, through exploration of divine methods known as direct contact with the Source. None of these are unusual phenomenon. They are how you learn to recognize and use precisely the skills you have. All this comes from awakening the divine in you. The practices help you to express an experience. The teachings are in tune with spiritual transcendence. These very beliefs unite the cosmos, deities, human beings, and destiny. Let wisdom come to you, as it is sent from the Source. Practice every day and illumination will follow.

Everything is perceived through knowing oneself and the essentials of Nature's elements. We use ritual systems because we want our mind to think independently. No longer are we conditioned by dogma that don't serve a purpose. Upon reaching a certain level of knowledge and spiritual maturity, our conscious thoughts are replaced by a full comprehension of the situation, seeing everything in its true nature. We are the recipients of divine energy. Truly you are reaching the full awakening of liberation. You're part of an activity that is shaping all aspects of your consciousness. The steps that you have made will lead you to discover the knowledge that resides in your subconscious.

Explore Your Sacred Truth

How to Unlock Your True Nature

Our subconscious is powerful and sophisticated. It is adaptive, smart, and creative. Simultaneously, the subconscious mind can lead you to make many subtle inquires without limitations. Ideas come to us as the subconscious uses an objective thought process. Unlike our conscious state in which we focus on one item at a time, the subconscious deals with several different processes at once. You will have the full power you need to take the initiative regarding your life. Spiritual practices center on integrating the nature of subconscious processes into daily life. And as I mentioned earlier, learning stillness is key. Two separate dimensions merge as you learn how to use the subconscious mind. Not only do you better understand the nature of cause and effect, awareness grows.

The very essence of human beings is in their consciousness. Scientists now recognize the subconscious as a unique gift to use and share. It is the portal to higher realms. By getting to know your subconscious, your spiritual comfort will increase and you will go deeper into the core of yourself. Now you can merge into oneness with Source and all the energy that comes from the Divine. The Divine is guiding you to self-understanding. I call this experience the pathway to the moment because it teaches you integrity of the soul and how to use it in the Now. This is how universal law works. It is alive and configuring the subconscious with divine abilities that are guiding you in the direction of divine awareness.

When your subconscious emerges into oneness, your inner energy shifts. It's so fluid, your instincts and intuition become your encyclopedia. This is not to be undervalued. Decisions can be made with much more ease on your part. Wisdom motivates you, not ignorance! You haven't noticed till now that courage is your nature. You chose to be part of a spiritual revolution. This trip leads to personal development and a journey to the inner soul. Now your subconscious is guiding you towards greater stability and the opportunity to gain access to higher consciousness. Fear not, you will receive the assistance you need, whether it is from the divine realm or people.

What people forget is that the universe breathes. Yes, it is full of life! And that is how all this is possible! When its elements are used correctly, universal law becomes extremely powerful. The messages integrate through the subconscious releasing a series of subtle solutions. Think of it as a broadcast of interpretations. Some call these experiences universal recognition. The Divine hears your call. As this happens, spirituality begins to play a dominant role in your life and you become the raw material of achievement. Look at yourself at the beginning of a journey, where everything is possible!

'Move forward with confidence' is your new motto! As you become more comfortable, ingenuity and open-mindedness expand to your subconscious. Levels of the subconscious are merging and overlapping with consciousness. In this state some people experience extrasensory seeing, hearing, touching, even smells. This series of stages is so absorbing that you become free of space and time. Don't rationalize your experiences. Just go with them. As you learn to decipher the messages, the realization that you can improve any situation you face becomes evident. Your spiritual side will be abundantly fed, and you will understand what is best for you on the path to inner enlightenment.

Spirituality has been engulfed by centuries of culture, yet in our era it fits into our contemporary lifestyle fluidly. It is up to you to have an open mind and to show empathy and forgive. Living in sustained spiritual awareness is the driving force that grounds you. I would like you to take a moment to reflect on these words that Deepak Chopra said in an interview: "The soul is the core of your being. Your mind is in your soul. The whole universe is part of your soul, and your soul is part of the universal consciousness.". This is the essential teaching in discovering the true self. To connect with Divinity is an extraordinary inner fulfillment.

Everything in the universe runs under universal law. It is by aligning with universal law that the connection is made to the flow of Creation. Think of it as the law of logic. Mind expansion is to be in silence and absorb the messages coming to you. What you are creating is a sacred bond between your soul and the Oneness. By unlocking your capabilities you can rely on your personal interpretations rather than the opinions of others. You can realize all your dreams. But first you must know yourself . You have more potential than you believe. I am only guiding you to discover it and use it. Spirit is calling you directly to awaken your divine birthright and your subconscious is sending messages to your brain to begin the process! It is saying, Step into the truth of awakening. The energies from other dimensions teach you how to interpret the meaning of the hidden messages you receive. It is a path of change—not a physical one, but a rebalancing of your subconscious mind.

As you connect with the world of energy you begin to take great steps forward. This is how you learn to connect to your "superior" spirit and become your highest form of self. Your spirit resides in the world of the Source. It not the solid world as we know it. It is the world where Creation begins. There time as we know it doesn't exist and you see beyond interpretations. From this world you can bring what you require in the physical world into manifestation. Nothing is hidden from your view.

This is how you find the God that is within you. Be mindful of what you are experiencing. You will be able to fit all the pieces together. Listen to what your intuition is saying to you. It's directing you to what you have to do.

You play a very important role on this Earth. Divine guidance is leading you on your journey. You have every right to work with your divine birthright. You will receive both the emotional and spiritual help you need to reach each new level. There are many diverse ways of connecting to the divine realm. No matter which one is your calling, start by letting the power flow from within. Accept with gentleness that you are moving in a new direction. You soul is opening up to new dimensions and portals, to where your higher self exists within Creation. Keep yourself focused when practicing and learn to let go of your doubts and fear. By continually expanding your true self you are allowing yourself to be all you can be! Blessed be.

VIII

The Mysterious Unknown and Understanding Its Spiritual Beauty

There Is Nothing Mysterious About It At All

PEOPLE HAVE ALWAYS been intrigued by the mystery that surrounds the "Unknown." The search to find answers about the mysterious Unknown has led people to many revelations. Even if you pretend to be unaffected by what people say and think about it, your mind can't help but wonder what it all means and why each person discovers a different truth. Instead of making the subject complex or confusing, let's approach it differently. I would like to say to you, forget everything you were taught on the matter! Let's explore the simple beauty of what the Unknown really means.

It is essential that you have your own experience and understanding of what some may call a phenomenon. Think of it as both the most special and the most ordinary development. To do so, you have to learn to understand the Divine from your true self. When your mind expands in its thought process everything becomes simple to understand. You are the very seed of manifestation. By trusting your intuition, you are more open to receive. As you grow more and more tuned in, what began as an imperceptible process becomes so clear that you can see things as they really are. It's a spiritual reality that infiltrates the reality of the everyday world . Your spiritual

The Mysterious Unknown and Understanding Its Spiritual Beauty

development is progressing and the way you view things is changing.

You now are going to learn how to access the "power from within" that will help you to reach a new spiritual level, change the way you think about cause and effect, and undoubtedly be like a catalyst. You will have a different definition of the world outside your body and the world that resides within your soul. Transformations in both spheres are taking place and you are discovering how living in harmony in these worlds brings stability. This is how you find the hidden depths of yourself. Only you have the capacity and ability to understand the mechanisms and subtleties that are unique to your inner self. Millions of people have found peace and solace by opening themselves up to what many refer to as the heavenly.

The purpose of discussing spirituality and its intricate systems is to educate. There are many facets to developing yourself. I would like you to have a basic knowledge of the process in order for you to grow in a productive way, one that allows you to think logically, especially as you begin your journey; one that addresses the most fundamental question of all: Who am I? As a seeker the answers you are searching for should not be ready-made; they should come to you from your soul. You are awakening a great self-discovery that is teaching you to absorb the understanding of the things that cross your path. Understanding the Divine may not be mysterious, but it does work in unique ways. You can master spiritual activities if you learn to adapt. You have the opportunity to make something meaningful out of the divine energy that is part of you. New spiritual experiences will occur to you giving you a new way of looking at things you experience. More precisely, you will have the tools to reach a greater wisdom in you. Question everything! If you don't, how will you understand and know what feels right for you? Your thoughts and actions will push you to dig deeper into your spiritual nature causing an eruption of unexpected and extraordinary fulfillment in your soul. The universe is yours and flows in oneness with you. These are the things that the Unknown brings to you when you surrender to it.

Contemplate and find the answer to this question: As a spiritual being, how open to the Unknown am I willing to be? This question can seem a little intimidating, but the reality is, it is simple. And while it is true the Creator who is our Source is distinct from us, we were created to be part of Its divine energy. The truth to your question lies in the knowledge you will receive from your soul. There are thousands of fibers that connect us in coexistence with higher energies. Some we may question because we have been conditioned to do so. Trust in the fact that the divine forces that surround you are creative and will teach you in the simplest ways so you will understand. You are emerging with the meaning of Creation.

The resurrection of your mind began the minute you said yes to believing. This is how you will be able to increase self-awareness. Even when the sublime presents itself to you, nothing is beyond your comprehension when you are clear in thought. You are building a relationship between the Source, yourself, and the universe. Infinite possibilities are available to you. To put it simply, you are divine and the power is in you to release your divinity! Once you decide to acknowledge that you have divine power within you, you become grounded and centered. Your connection with the Divine is like a braid, one that is woven between the spiritual and human levels. Unconsciously you will become more receptive to the vibrations you receive. You will grow enormously as a spiritual person.

The Mysterious Unknown and Understanding Its Spiritual Beauty

Freedom to be divine is your birthright! You are being asked to face something that is invisible but very real. Your inner spirit is colossal when you develop it. At present your inner self is merging with natural divine forces, leading you to experience a true awakening of your soul. You'll learn what it means to be in synch with all of creativity and your true self. You will live and fulfill your spiritual quest. The Divine will merge with your subconscious and teach you how to use this newfound wisdom in everyday life. You are ready to move in a new direction that wraps you in the light of divinity and keeps you balanced in the world. You'll discover that what you thought was hidden was always there and is now unveiling itself to you. This will be a turning point in your life. You are embarking on the inner path of the soul, a mystical journey to the Unknown.

This is a period of preparation for you. You have your spiritual enlightenment to fulfill in a culture that doesn't always agree on spiritual matters. I believe that is the biggest reason that the Unknown becomes problematic to people. When I was first learning about spirituality, I had to overcome doubt and fear. The ego mind is fill of trickery. This is to be expected. But as you take the steps to develop yourself further, it becomes easier to trust the natural forces of the unseen worlds. Describing it is not comparable to what you will feel. It's as if you can taste and smell the sublime. Transparent and exact concepts come to you to help you distinguish this path from the previous one you were on. In this time, you will have Source energy guiding you.

How can your true self come to the surface if you are afraid to discover it? Awareness grows out of cognition. The only way to discover your truth is to explore what is hidden within you. This you can only achieve by spiritual practice. It is like holding a solid brick of gold. Brightness is everywhere. You have to invite

Explore Your Sacred Truth

it into your life. Most of all you have to believe in it. And you begin to believe by practicing. That is how you feel the forces of energy flowing through you. Finally your eyes are unveiled and you see the full effect they have on you. Nobody but you can feel this. At this time, I advise you to flow with the emotions and experiences that will definitely arise. Don't be afraid to transcend your old self and become who you really are.

As you connect with the forces that govern the universe they will rapidly infiltrate your mind, causing a ripple effect to occur deep inside your core. At this time you have the opportunity to access hidden knowledge. As a person seeking truth you have the advantage because you now are the master over what happens in your life. If you sit in stillness, you will realize what your existence on this planet means. We each have a purpose and yours will be shown to you. When we are not on a spiritual path, we almost never find the answer. But when we are receptive and respect what we learn about cause and effect and universal law, all is within our reach.

ACCEPTING THE TEACHINGS

When you accept these teachings, your need for spiritual purity will be filled and you will learn that the Unknown is really quite familiar. In order to find union between you and the Divine, call on the universe. It is constantly creating new things. Let it be a source of strength for you. This is how you draw guidance from your divine essence and Source energy. You have to respect the systematic levels in your spiritual growth in order to better benefit from universal law. There is an old saying: "When you learn to live as you truly are, you become your best self." No truer words were ever spoken. You are courageous to be you and don't you forget it!

The Mysterious Unknown and Understanding Its Spiritual Beauty

Use direct communication as you were taught in the previous chapters to bridge the known and unknown worlds. You may be surprised to learn that eighty percent of the world's population believes in the potential of the spiritual Unknown, or to put it simply, the supernatural. We call this spiritual intelligence, and our bodies and mind share in the benefits of it. Did you know that immediately upon connecting with the Divine our overall mental and physical health is sounder? Why? Because we are in oneness with all of Creation and are part of the bigger universe. We know that we interconnect with all that exists and that we are spiritually responsible for who we want to be. You make the choice to live your inner truth. No one else can do it for you.

Divine incarnation is an opportunity to live a life with purpose. It helps you get rid of what no longer serves you and work with the things that add to your divine well-being. Spiritual guides and higher beings are in the background aiding you on your journey. The spiritual Unknown teaches you to see the deeper side of who you are. The Unknown is allowing you to tap into the Source energy that sustains all living things. Your subconscious is interacting with spiritual dimensions and you are beginning to see things as they really are. Each step of the way your soul expands into total union with the Divine that dominates the two worlds.

When a person takes the initiative to explore their spirituality they are embarking on a journey to discover their inner connection with the Oneness and Creation. It has nothing to do with a person's religious beliefs. Too many times the two get confused. You are not trading one for another. You are on a journey to unlock your mind from the constraints of being conditioned. It is the pinnacle of learning how to think independently, the opposite of being told what to think. We use a structure to help us make our practices more productive. This is how we comprehend what our psyche is teaching us. The goal is to understand how living from our core values transforms us.

When we begin our path, the essence of our understanding is like an embryo. We have to nurture what is happening to us so the embryo can grow and develop healthily. It is very interesting to observe ourselves as we dig deep into our true nature. When you embrace the process, it allows you to go very deep. Then you are releasing yourself into unconditioned consciousness.

Each of us is made of energy. Energy is constantly moving. Therefore, do not be mechanical in the way you think, but make the effort to be present and awake. The energy that you are made of can sustain you spiritually. You start off on your path when you begin to train and awaken your consciousness and experience the truth of yourself. Let us observe even further how the world is affected by this phenomenon:

Worldwide, people are becoming increasingly vulnerable to war, poverty, an unsteady food supply, and global warming, all caused by humankind. We are fighting our way through these obstacles. The good news is the divine realm is causing a shift to occur. Globally the Divine is feeding people spiritually, and it is causing a resurgence in awakening. I call it a "healthy" energy that is being sent. For the people who open up to receiving this energy, realization is taking place from within. Multiple elements from forces that cannot be seen are creating change. The forces may at first be "unknown" to you, but the message is clear. It is calling for the spiritually inclined to wake up out of sleep and for humanity as a whole to start living "intelligently." The Divine is creating what I call a "Picasso." Our Source energy works in a beautifully woven intricate system of oneness whose force we benefit from.

The Mysterious Unknown and Understanding Its Spiritual Beauty

The same is true of Nature as a whole. We possess the elements within to connect expansively with the universe. By allowing spiritual birth to take place we become naked in thought, and we can see how the transformation happens. This is a working system to awaken your spiritual nature. The more we identify with our divine DNA, the more we become effective in withering the ego. When this occurs you will have good balance between your actions and thoughts. It becomes obvious to you that it is better to follow an intelligent spiritual path that surpasses the previous path you were on that was full of conditioning. Now you think with logically. The goal is to be able to use your intuition regularly. Your instincts are an extraordinary tool to use and now is your chance. Each of us has a role on the planet and in the spiritual realm. These worlds come together when you ask them to in order for you to claim your divine birthright.

You're taking an inner journey to discover who you are. To do so you'll use the ancient techniques you learned to uncover the beauty and peace that can always be found within you. The Divine is giving you guidance in achieving coordination of self and Spirit. It is a path of inner harmony that is achieved through methods that, if used wisely, are practical every step of the way. In other words, they are a form of superior logic. Everything in spirituality is related to learning how to expand our consciousness. We do this in order to experience truth for ourself.

The whole cosmos is in constant movement, continuously creating and expanding. These are the same forces that are referred to as mysterious or unknown to us. But you are beginning to understand that the beautiful revelation you are experiencing is real as you become able to discern through divine senses that the readjustments you make have a positive impact in your life. You are being placed in is a position to master the ability to evolve into a higher being. That is why I keep stressing to look for the signs. They are being shown to you. Life is about balance. And when you are in this state your energy is much more grounded and centered.

The universe is asking you to take a leap of faith. It is clearing your energy of any experiences that may be slowing your progress. You do hold in you the strength to do what needs to be done. Start by knowing the potential of who you really are. Don't let the human mind limit you. Continue to practice and expand your subconscious mind. Keep yourself focused on the goal. Spirit is working with you to make the space you are meant to have. Now is the time to begin using your gifts in your own service. You are entering a period of new inspirations and self-discovery. The beauty is that you are able to explore this on your own. Meditation is the route to knowing. When you do it , it eliminates dependency and the mind can breathe. The Source is creativity. Don't change the beauty that lies inside of you. You are skyrocketing to your highest potential.

Embrace the shift that is occurring in you because you are entering the world of higher energies. You will most definitely understand them better. When you enter this world you always receive a teaching. Your instincts will direct you well. There is nothing egotistical about knowing your own worth. By allowing yourself to be truly seen you are taking a necessary step toward experiencing life through the Source. The shift we are speaking of is from thinking to awareness. In this transitional period, you will have to adapt to a consciousness that is different from the one you have known. You will have to exercise a great finesse of mind in order to appreciate the repercussions from this shift.

Believing is a good start because with acceptance comes many possibilities, and it helps you to begin to work out of your spirit.

The Mysterious Unknown and Understanding Its Spiritual Beauty

A bond is being formed within you that brings with it new spiritual ambitions. No longer will your thinking be sabotaged by a limiting mindset. Rather your mind is continually going to transform into new paradigms of thinking. Once that happens everything as you've known it suddenly looks very different. You must not be intimidated by the other side of life, the one of the divine realm. You are having a revelation that is in fact linked to your destiny. A spiritual awakening will benefit your life and bring change to the soul. There are many of us who already have experienced these changes and can attest to the power of spiritual values. In my own life it was a period of radical change, one that taught me how to use my power so it flows from within and not by force. By understanding that you are a divine being you recognize you are on a guided path. More will be accomplished by you and you will have much more peace in your life. Have gratitude that you are being blessed with a divine flow that opens your energy in an omnipotent way. The time has come for you to illuminate your path. The divine DNA you posses is very special. This is the road to greater clarity. You are now able to express outwardly your true being. I suggest you continue to follow the light in front of you instead of the darkness that is now behind you.

You have so much to offer this planet by paying attention to the spiritual messages you receive. You will instinctively know how to fulfill your role. Remember you are on an ultimate journey to discover how the deepest essence of who you are determines how you live your life. You are joining together with other spiritual people, Nature, and the divine realm. This is your larger reality. You are setting yourself apart from the ordinary and inviting sacred truth into your life. You are learning about how everything in Nature and energy affects you, and you're realizing that your energy is separate from your body. So you begin to question what is behind it all.

You may be asking yourself. Why am I living a conditioned lifestyle if I am a divine being? What is oneness with Creation? What kind of energy do I share with the Source ? Why does religion play a role? These are not uncommon things to ask yourself. At times the questions can be more worrying than reassuring. Let me begin by saying you've chosen to take the journey to Earth before. That is why you are infused with divine DNA from birth that is meant to activate your spiritual intellect and keep a flowing connection between the divine realm and you, if you choose that it do so. People who are spiritual choose to develop the relationship with Divinity rather than ignore it. It becomes a quest to establish a peaceful inner balance. So the search begins to find answers that make sense to you rather than to rely on the ones that have been imposed on you. Globally people want to break with the things that no longer serve their well-being. As you let go and tune in to receive the messages that are being sent to you, you begin to understand how creation works and its influence on all living things. Then a wonderful event happens when you realize the Source of Creation is continuously generating energy that is life-giving. Most of all you understand that developing spiritually is about you, not your religious beliefs. In fact, when you are spiritual, you are a better you! When you put it all together you suddenly say to yourself, I understand that the unknown is really many facets of interconnecting knowledge. This helps you understand the beauty of your divine nature.

IX

Individuality and Spirituality

Embrace Your True Individualism

WHEN I WAS discovering the inner science of what it means to embrace your true individualism, I simply found myself in an intriguing maze that caused a metamorphosis of my entire being. The experience for each person is different; nonetheless, it is life-altering. I am referring to a shift of your spiritual nature and your own individuality. It fascinates me to see the amazing reactions people have when they make the connection between the two.

The purpose of individuality and spirituality is to discover who and what your true nature is and to live a balanced and fulfilling life based on fundamental principles. It's not based on what religion you believe in. I feel it is necessary to bring this point to your attention. Your religion is sacred to you and a source of strength to draw from. What spirituality is suggesting to you is that you let the god in yourself come forth. Too many people are conditioned to fear God, and that shouldn't be the case. In fact we are divine beings with extraordinary abilities. Most people have been conditioned to believe that they are inferior beings, and that is simply not true. It is time for you to become empowered with divine essence.

The Divine wants you to discover who you are as a spiritual being and as an individual who is independent of conditioning.

Explore Your Sacred Truth

When I speak of conditioning in this context I am speaking on different levels starting from day-to-day living to the spiritual consistency you seek in your life, and everything else in between. It is an opportunity to come into your own as who you truly are. Let's face it, when we are not grounded we become bogged down with mind fog. Everyone wants to find their spot in life, and the best way to do it is to become "inspired." It is that inspiration that gives you the passion to continue on your path and not the path of others. You leave the cocoon, become the caterpillar, and you are finally free to fly as the butterfly. The beauty of this experience is that from the ordinary, you become extraordinary. Mind, body, and soul are in complete union with each other and working as one.

You are thinking, what does she mean by conditioning? And how does it relate to me? The truth is each of us at some point is influenced in how we think. Past or present, it doesn't matter; it happens. Most of the time we don't notice the effect it has on us because we are unaware and living without seeing. Each of us has a right to live according to divine laws and discover within those laws what choices we can make. We instinctively become aware that there is so much more to our existence than we were taught. We are able to examine things in a new light, knowing the lessons we receive help us to understand better who we are. You are stepping into yourself in a comfortable way. As you begin to live this way you are unconsciously molding your individuality to your true self. The spiritual journey is also a personal path to discovery, and it covers a full lifetime. It leads to having a capable and free mind, which is needed if we are to live steadfastly in our life process. It is an acceptance of who you are and the way you balance all you undertake. Everyone on this planet wants to feel complete in their own skin. When you think with spiritual intelligence, you make the wisest choices for yourself.

By understanding your needs as an individual you create harmony in yourself. You are reaching another stage on your journey to enlightenment. It is what I call "developing inside your individuality." This is how you eliminate any lingering circumstances that prevented you from advancing before you became "aware." When I speak in these terms I am referring to a deep connection that is created inside your being and is extended to your outside aura. It is a total reorganization of your principles and ideas. This is the perfect time to learn how to use your inner energy to influence who you really are.

The fact is that your inner journey is how you identify your true self. And your true self leads you to intensify actively your spiritual quest. The two are linked with each other. This is how you discover how to completely modify the course of your life. Don't you like the idea of having the mental freedom to be your own person and spiritual guru? As a rule, people tend to forget that they are unique and can make a contribution to life's processes. Going on a life-changing quest means you no longer take any moments for granted and you look at life as full of new possibilities. Divine consciousness is the choice you made to become aware of the steps you need to take to make your journey. To be your own person and to have spiritual power is to accept who you are. You will learn and grow from these experiences on every level. I call it a lesson in how to live from the essence of your true soul. You are the driver steering the course of your life.

It's a conscious choice to use the knowledge from your inner powers to move forward. As you step beyond the physical and let your mind expand, you are lifting yourself up to your higher being. These are the reasons you should never say you are too busy for meditation, because meditation helps your consciousness to flow into Oneness. This is how you keep the balance between the two worlds you slip in and out of. You are a being in transition and rebirth, a being that is rooted in a foundation of vibrational energy that is carried through the universe and focusing on a better you who has the confidence and ability to live by divine law.

People want to know what it means to be Spiritual. The answer is simple: Being spiritual is walking a path that leads to oneness with universal law. Each person experiences it differently, but one thing it is definitely about is an inner path leading to different places in the psyche so that they may grow abundantly and according to divine principle. One thing it is not about is religion. It is about living in the Now and how to be a fulfilled person, one who uses the universal elements to discover the essence of their own beauty from inside. It is a connection between Creation and Nature and how we evolve and coexist within them. A renewal is being offered to you. Embrace it with a vigorous attitude. There is no need ever to have to turn your attention to the past again. I would like you to think in these terms and say to yourself, 'My spiritual knowledge shapes my quest for all the endeavors I will embark on.'

To really benefit from all of this you will have to take the time to make full use of what you have learned and practice the rituals so that favorable developments can take root. Now would be a good time to dispose of anything that is superficial and holding you back. You must do so in order to surpass yourself and accomplish a goal that few people manage to achieve in a lifetime. Challenge yourself and train your subconscious to attain a higher spiritual evolution. The intention to begin something combined with movement produces an action. It is a chance to be yourself in a spiritual process which is wonderfully bold and liberating. You are a spirit of energy and you are free to make your own choices. For far too long people believed themselves to be ordinary instead of realizing that they have infinite powers to change anything in the zone they create. It is time to live by the higher principles of self-worth . You are an immeasurable source of consciousness when you learn how to access it.

The only person who can make the necessary effort toward positive results for you in the areas of personal and spiritual well-being is you. This is making a life change that is consistent with the principles you are living by. It is a time when you can honestly say to yourself that your human integrity and discernment are working in oneness. A feeling of freedom engulfs you when you are working in union with the forces of divine law. The Divine is working in harmony and in your favor to help you reach your highest potential. It's a moment of truth when you feel it, and that's when you reclaim ownership of your soul and a great liberty. As your energy becomes centered and grounded you can meet all your needs with clarity. Your spiritual needs and your true being are balanced. Improving your life depends on your understanding of yourself and others. Really, everything you are doing to improve yourself contributes to a process of continual learning.

We travel on this path to discover the deepest part of our person. We are not talking about a person's personality. A personality can be modified to fit in to its environment. For example, you may change your clothing when starting a new job so you're dressing like the others in your workplace. Or you can start to speak like the people around you if you are in a new place. When a person does these things they are modifying aspects of their personality to feel comfortable in a particular environment.

Explore Your Sacred Truth

Real comprehension begins for us when we understand that our personality is different from our inner being. Think of yourself as a human machine that is transmitting from inside its being to the outside atmosphere. It will be necessary to look inside of you because you alone can face your own image and redefine it. We want to maintain a healthy balance between our psyche and spiritual needs. This is how we generate good energy around us. It is very important, since energy is continuously moving, to keep our energies positive, which keeps our consciousness awake and aware. These are the energies that are directing you to connect with empowerment of self. All the experiences that you are having are leading you to walk the path that fits you. Take time each day to keep the channels open between you and your spiritual side so the divine flow can keep moving .

Throughout the book I have been guiding as to how to develop the tools that you are born with so you can use them to access the Divine in you and take in new information and teachings. The principles presented here are to help you process the changes that are going to take place in you. I explained earlier that each person has a different experience and no two journeys are the same. Those experiences can be subtle or extremely intense; it is different for each person. The teachings in this book are guiding you to a point of entry to reach a higher level of consciousness. I am trying to help open your mind to the many facets that are involved in the process of learning the relationship between you and spirituality. Metaphorically, this is a guide to the entry point to spiritual doorways so you may step through them with confidence and experience the journey with an open mind.

This book was written to share knowledge in order for you to challenge your mind and beliefs . I want you to understand that this is your journey and I am only a guide helping you to open the channel within you. The journey is for you to live and experience. As I guide you, I like to emphasize letting go of fear and being open to the experience. I do this so that you can focus on yourself rather than what you think is expected of you. It is a process to truly discover your inner person with no inhibitions or insecurities. The teachings inspire you to live in harmony with all that is in your spiritual and individual nature. My journey led me to discover things so deep within me that when I opened the channels, I finally was able to connect with the real me.

The journey is different for each of us, but emotionally humans experience the same feelings such as love, hope , concern about family and financial matters, and fear. It is natural to the human spirit to want to improve. But the global epidemic of uncertainty has been sweeping over humanity fiercely in the last decade. People are searching to live in a way that brings them comfort and spiritual stability. This is what the journey of being attuned to higher levels of consciousness means. It is an interconnection that brings all the elements we are discussing together. It's as if the universe were calling you to use your journey to gain knowledge through your experiences. These writings are the roots that nourish and teach you as you are having experiences from the Divine. This knowledge is for the people who are seeking to find a sincere relationship to spirituality and core principles. Throughout the centuries sacred principles of universal law have been used to preserve these practices. They teach you to go beyond the usual spiritual approach and outside the physical body in order to acquire complete knowledge. This is not blind destiny; it is the innermost connection with the subconscious and Oneness. It is the power to change from within, useful to anyone practicing spiritual traditions. When you know yourself, you come to know the universe and its gods, and most importantly, the Source of Creation.

Every person is different in their passions and the desires they have. We who practice these principles seek intelligence from within rather than allowing the ego to fill us with false projections. Spiritual practices function like everything else in existence through the laws of Nature. It is these laws that allow divine principles to enter into your life so you can live in your true state of being. This is how you achieve development of all the energies from the natural world and access the inner dimensions of the soul and what exists beyond the physical. We don't look at these practices as concepts. We know them as sacred and ancient knowledge that has been taught to humanity from the beginning of time.

At this point you have come to know how the structured exercises help you and expand your mind when exploring your spiritual nature. The experiences you have are unique to you and important for your development. And because as a human you can make free choices it is you who controls your growth. It takes a lot of strength to go within and discover yourself, and we all go through changes as we do. I have a friend who refers to the journey as a vinaigrette. When she said it a light bulb flashed and I realized it was brilliant to describe it this way. You see, when your being and spiritual side fuse together it is a complete harmony. But sometimes on the journey to get there we take a step forward and then backwards. When this happens people often "freeze.".Understand that being spiritual does not mean you don't hit bumps in the road. On my journey I was making strides moving forward, and then I came up against a blockage. I knew I had to be the one to push forward and work past it. Working past natural human tendencies was the only way to free myself. It will be the same for you too! People choose how they go in and out of experience. Sometimes we consciously tend not to listen to our inner voice; but Spirit knows we'll get back on the journey. I bring this to your attention so when it happens to you it doesn't create a major issue. You will work past it and walk the path that is meant for you. Your understanding of this knowledge lets you submerge fully into discovery of yourself and still have choices. I emphasize these points because sometimes the information we receive isn't always accurate for growth and I want to set the record straight. This is why you will always here gurus say, keep the consciousness awake at all times, live in the moment. These are the essentials on your journey.

Reflection helps us to understand what is happening to us on our journey. This is how we get to know the relationship we have with Spirit. It's like a picture where your mind can relate to the events that are taking place and adjust accordingly. It is important to take time to be alone and give your inner self an opportunity to connect with your higher self. People who are practicing have to do so at a pace that blends all of what is natural in a way that is fluid. When you come into self and Spirit everything that concerns you is processed in a psychologically and socially correct frame of mind. It is a time to congratulate yourself because you have reached a stage that allows you to manage your emotions astutely. Prudence in all matters will bring you the strength to make the right choices.

SPIRITUAL PILGRIM OF BALANCE

As spiritual beings we focus and reflect on what is happening in the present. People who live their lives based on universal law undoubtedly handle their lives better than others. Even when faced with difficult moments they instinctively know that everything passes. As balance takes over it is easier to learn that life is a process of events. That is why we learn to look at things as if they are in motion. Understand the journey is a pilgrimage, and new life awaits you as you enter into each stage. You will know how to achieve spiritual and interpersonal relationships with balance. Spiritual guides are nudging you forward to reach your full potential. The knowledge you are receiving helps you to understand who you are. Old karma is leaving you and new energy is replacing it.

Throughout the book I speak of connecting with your true self and how important it is in order to live a spiritual life. Now would be a perfect time to let your spiritual intelligence guide you in thought as we move into discussion of the subject. To go inside the deepest part of your core and discover the person you are is one of the most courageous things you will ever do. It is only when you know your true being that you can progress to a state of full acceptance of yourself. From a spiritual perspective this is one of the most difficult parts of the spiritual journey. You will have to demonstrate a realistic attitude to face the new reality you will most definitely live. To really know yourself is to face the darkest parts of you so the light inside you can emerge. It is a time when you may feel vulnerable to the emotion that is rising in you. Your awareness will help you reexamine all the qualities that make up who you are. This is a reassessment of yourself. When you are in the process you will experience moments of great revival and other moments of anguish; at times they will come simultaneously.

People tend to get thrown off course when they hear the word "darkness." Understandably so. No one wants to acknowledge they have dark places inside of them. The first thought that comes into a person's mind when they hear the word is that they

Individuality and Spirituality

have little or no spiritual light in them. This is a normal reaction and one that is easily controlled with intelligent thinking. Nobody else has your divine DNA and that is why you are the only one who can discover what your true essence is. Think of it as a detoxification of anything that is hindering your growth. You alone are able to bring any hurts that were never healed in your life to the surface. Discovering your true being means that you are willing to feel your emotions as they are and confront any uncertainties. Because the emotions are coming from within it is best to make progress in stages. Don't be afraid; you have all the energy you need to eliminate whatever is hindering you. Spirituality is a step-by-step process and everyone that enters the light is also a warrior of darkness. First you have to recognize in your mind that the light is ever-present in you. Release what no longer serves you, free it into the light, and the energy from it will push you forward. This is how you begin the passage toward opening up to your highest potential. You are laying your spiritual foundation and taking control of who you are. Relationships are built on faith and trust in both the physical and spiritual worlds. You can learn about the core of your being and not be in denial about your mistakes. The moment you become aware of what you need to do in order to live as you are, a feeling of vindication fills you and you are no longer a slave to conditioned mind patterns. You are now connecting with the Source of Creation instead of listening to dogma.

Remember you are now walking a path to true discovery. This is a time when your emotions will have a powerful effect over your mind. Learning how to control your inner self is essential, especially when you are faced with anything that is going to challenge you and may dampen your aura. You are aiming to learn how to control challenges so they don't fill your head and consume you. The best approach is to come back to center because when you do, you can hear your inner voice guiding you. Listen to the voice that is inside you because it will help you to reach the right decisions. As you are coming into your own you'll notice that you're developing on an intellectual level so that you understand you are being accompanied by the Divine. You are simply using energy when necessary to overcome resistance. Rumi wrote, "I have come to drag you out of yourself." When I was writing this chapter those words kept ringing in my ear. They're very powerful words. When you emerge from within by using discipline and intuition, everything from inside of you is revealed within your mind. As your mind evolves to a state of discipline you cease to believe that you are better than the next person, nor do you believe you are inferior. You are creating a sacred space where you can be naked in your thoughts without fear. This allows you to appreciate the similarities you have with the Divine and also to respect the differences. Your mind is learning how to leave behind the insecurities that can hinder potent human development. There is no other way to know who you are than to go deep inside your core and explore from within. It is the only way to true discovery of the person you want to live as on your journey. It all goes back to receiving knowledge from experience and continually practicing what you learn and developing it to your fullest potential. From your observations and analysis of living in harmony with Nature's forces you can fine-tune your being into the flow of divine life. Being at one with your soul is the ultimate feeling of peace.

When you first made the decision to take this journey you began to transform to a higher level of consciousness; but since you were just at the entry gate you didn't fully understand the effects of the changes that were taking place in you. Now that you are aware of what is happening to you, be like a grid, or a vacuum tube of energy. The energy you are harnessing holds logical and spiritual information. This is a major turning point in your life; you must learn how to balance these energies. Energy is alive and it continually moves in and out of us quickly when we don't direct it. You want to learn how to keep the light inside you. The easiest way to do it is by keeping your intentions clear and by staying grounded. What you think and feel has it effects on your energy. You don't want to release it unconsciously or let it be taken away from you.

Yes, I said "taken away." We must not let others drain the energy we have. When a light surrounds you people want what you possess. Most of the time it isn't intentional; it is just a natural reaction for others to want to be around people who exude pure energy. This is when you use awareness to control how much energy you release without depleting your supply. Remember, you are like a magnet and you are going to attract things and people to you. The wise person understands that not everyone's energy is the same and good to be around. You want to preserve the energy you have and take care of it to stay in balance with the elements of the universe. Through spiritual intelligence and a logical thought process your mind is able to understand these natural laws and wait for the moments that bring the most opportunity to act and go forward.

It is a fact that people develop differently. Once you decide to go on this quest it becomes a life-changing process, one that takes perseverance on your part to see it though to the end. This is a journey that requires you to be judicious and practical in your dealings. People want different things from their spiritual paths in terms of what makes them happy. Develop at your own pace and don't compare yourself to others. The fantastic thing about coming in to yourself is that you are using intelligence to make decisions and you are not relying on what has been told to you by others and conditioned your way of thinking. This type of logic demands courage because you are stepping into what feels like the unknown, but in realty it is self-discovery. Once you acclimatize yourself to the vibrations that come from the supernatural realms you will begin to "ease up" and embrace the natural order of the way things work. When we learn to stop underestimating what we are capable of doing we can learn how to express our true nature.

The beauty of the moment comes when you are in oneness. It could occur during a simple sunset, when you can feel that you are the sunset rather than the sunset is a separate object you're watching. It is about opening the window in the center of your soul and learning how to travel beyond the dimension you are currently in and into another. That is one of the reasons I keep stressing the importance of setting intention,, because I want you to understand fully your capabilities. This is the time to be pragmatic and allow manifestation to take place. Remember the connection between yourself and spirituality is about attaining life's goals and spiritually evolving simultaneously. You want to be in harmony and stay in a state of awareness. You can do this by listening to your intuition as it is guiding you.

Mostly what people want out of the human journey is to live a life that has balance. The world as we know it is in unrest, and the common goal of mankind is to live a peaceful existence. As a spiritual guide my mission has become to help people acknowledge and accept their own divine blue-print. I realize not everyone will choose to make the spiritual journey, but I would like to see as many people as possible learn about the options and explore the possibilities. It takes a great amount of

Individuality and Spirituality

strength to go on a journey of the soul. For those who want to go beyond what is tangible, you are being guided to find common ground between yourself and higher consciousness. You will have the chance to leave human ignorance behind and live with purpose. Your spiritual and personal being are a project you undertake. They are interconnected and you have to be aware of their components so you don't compromise the relationship between self and the Divine. This is the path that connects you to Divine Spirit.

X

Consenting to the Journey

TAKING FLIGHT

YOU CAN TAKE what I write in two ways: as authority to be followed blindly, or you can use your spiritual intelligence to consider it and come to your own conclusions. If you just take it on my authority you will never grow, and you will be conditioning your mind to go along with the crowd. However, if you use intelligence and ask for spiritual guidance, the questions you have about your life path will be answered. That said, when you decide to use intelligence and logic your true journey will begin.

Think of each part of the journey as a cell that keeps dividing and growing. Remember, I said earlier that human wiring is an intricate system. The more you use this system and develop it, the more advanced it becomes. As you step into your true self you quickly realize that your thought process has to be flexible, because you are going to venture out of your comfort zone in a very exciting and untraditional way. When we take the mask off we are able to see behind it to our true self. We who are spiritual seekers learn how to overcome the fear that holds us back by expanding into subconsciousness. As we begin to change old thought patterns, we realize that purging the old ways is the only way to find ourselves from within.

Consenting to the Journey

To live in balance on this path you must not have any illusions about what the spiritual journey entails. You play the lead role in your life. The journey you are taking is one that allows you to live an intelligent lifestyle in which the choices and decisions you make are the wisest for the manner in which you live. You will have to be honest and ask yourself, what is it that I am seeking? You have made a choice to improve "you!" Many people don't know what to expect when approaching spiritual science, there are so many misconceptions. I'd like to guide you as to what it means when you say yes to the inner journey.

As spiritual beings we are aware that we are connected with the Source of the life-giving force. We elect to think smart and develop alongside the divine principle. Instead of conditioning ourselves to traditional ways, we learn how to process our decisions with logic. Our values are centered on ethics, morals, and humane virtues. As we venture further into our spiritual development, we become aware that we have a protective energy field around us. We start to feel the vibrations of energy and to become receptive to the divine sources that are surrounding us. The knowledge you are learning is ancient and has been practiced for centuries. It requires you to make changes and think expansively. Sometimes this is difficult, but if you continue onward with patience it is rewarding. Should you choose to go ahead on the spiritual journey, one thing you will definitely learn is to know yourself better on the conscious and subconscious levels.

The world and its people have come to know chaotic times. All human beings face the same triumphs and struggles, no matter what part of the world they live in. Instead of promoting chaos, spirituality teaches us a new understanding of the human element and how to have a fresh perspective on things. It teaches us how to optimize our development in order to live a more balanced lifestyle. Our beliefs are based on the everlasting Source of Creation and the natural order of elements. Religions of the world also originate from these. Remember, each person's journey encourages them to develop their spiritual nature with an open mind.

Most people do not believe they have divine and perfect identities, and they never take the opportunity to develop their tools. When this happens we most definitely lose insight of our true purpose and fail to realize humans are the most capable of all species of taking care of the Earth and its life force. When you live a life that is centered, you can expect to be more focused, balanced, and at one with yourself. You have clearer insight in making decisions and you learn to accept the energy flow in a natural sense. You're triumphant, and setbacks are how you gain wisdom and come to know the light source that is within you. Through personal development you instinctively are able to reach a new realization in your life. You are your own light, and that is a tremendous power in itself. When you look into yourself, you begin to want to manifest the knowledge you are learning in your way of living.   The spiritual path takes time and patience. Discovery and making the connection only come when a person is willing to make a commitment to finding their true purpose. You have to see the beauty of your own light first in order to understand the Source of life and the benefits that it has for you. If you allow yourself to receive and give, you begin to see your future path. Many people fail to realize that we as a species were given a unique soul that houses a brilliant mind. The spiritual path is a birthing path where you see the opportunity and become who you should be! Each person is designed as a unique masterpiece, and when you are willing to

Consenting to the Journey

look at yourself from the inside you learn to leave behind human ignorance a positive change begins to transform you and you automatically think on a higher intellectual level. You actually begin to reach levels at which your whole essence is on a mission to live in union with the laws that govern Nature. Your way of viewing things becomes clear and constructive. Your thoughts are channeled in an exchange of knowledge with higher dimensions. The steps you take on this path will lead you towards an inner transformation and discovering the meaning of your existence on Earth. In the beginning you might not be aware of the total effect it has on you; however, as time passes you will understand you have been given the wisdom you need to continue forward. Think of the positive change as entering new territory that will benefit your life.

You will be drawn to find what I call the "deep truth." It is an extraordinary achievement to discover your true self. Even if others do not understand your new goals, you should not doubt your potential. You will find that when you are on the spiritual path, you will build up an inflexible determination that will eventually bring a great satisfaction to your soul. This path is a new reality that opens up possibilities for you that you never dreamed of. When you spiritually evolve every area of your life improves. You will never go back to the way you used to live because now you clearly see the truth that humans are meant to live a spiritual existence. You and the universe are dwelling as one in truth and peace. You are entering a new phase of life which will bring you to your real calling.

Just as biodiversity strengthens natural systems, the diversity of the spiritual journey strengthens our human relations and encourages us to achieve our fullest potential in our individuality. Remember, you are the only one who can seek it out and search for it. That is why it is wise first to search within and find your true self . Only when you do this will you see the outside and reach your objective. In the end it will be your tenacity and perseverance that will lead you to become conscious of your true nature and help you to grow spiritually. When you are on the spiritual path, the universe will support you in all you do. When your senses are truly alive, there is an amazing amount of energy that awakens every one of your cells. This is the ultimate source of vitality, a vast realm of intelligence that goes beyond thought.

Making a Life-changing Decision

When you make the decision to consent to the journey of enlightenment, you are saying yes to finding inner peace and living in a harmonious balance with your true self. The journey teaches you how to listen from your core. This is the way you discover how to refine your senses and erase conditioning from your mind. At this level you are connecting within your "psychological depth." You are extremely alert without the excess baggage that fogs your thought process. It's a transformation of your mind into a state of total receptiveness in which the ego doesn't exist. This is the portal to transforming your consciousness into oneness with the universe's energies. Your mental skills are now being used in a way that will lead to the enrichment of your moral views. Conflicting emotions no longer exist; replacing them is a balance that is aligned with natural law.

Fulfilling your spiritual responsibility brings to you a power from within that merges with divine sources, naturally transforming your energy into self-empowerment. This newfound knowledge that you are receiving challenges culturally conditioned patterns. It is a psychological strength that encompasses you and it is quite real. Over time a new portal opens to you and allows a different life process to manifest. Don't let limiting conditioning of the mind hold you back from being who you truly are. A journey to self-discovery is not about becoming someone new; it is about connecting with and being the true self. You probably have already noticed that your thought process is changing, becoming more clear and concise.

Seeing and feeling the connection with the Source of Creation and the universe will keep your focus on the higher good and your energy in tune with your higher self. It is important to remember you are not alone when you are transitioning. There will be higher forces supporting you and giving you guidance as you need it. The guidance you receive can come in many forms. Look and listen for the messages and signs around you because they can be subtle. What you will be experiencing is what I call a perpetual regeneration of the mind, body, and soul. As your mind connects to the higher intellectual forces that are guiding you, you clearly see what is good or bad for you. You will not act blindly in the decisions you have to make. Your soul wants to get to a place where your spirituality and your true self are in balance with each other.

Along the way you will have questions. You'll be learning and discovering that the journey you're on is uniquely your own. Stay clear of expectations about what will happen. I mentioned previously that each person has a different journey and different gifts. The ultimate gift you can receive on this quest is to be who you truly are and to understand your own being. When your soul reaches this stage you will know the power that self-enlightenment brings to you. It is a journey that you pursue with consistency and prudence. This is how spiritual seekers regard their pursuit; it is the silent pulse that connects them to everything life and the universe have to offer.

Explore Your Sacred Truth

Once you enter into the marvelous world of inner enlightenment and familiarize yourself with the rituals that connect you to your higher self, you will begin to have detailed revelations. Such awakenings lead you to interpret logically the signs that are transmitted to you. As you develop these skills, you can approach all aspects of your life processes from a spiritually intelligent perspective. These processes are in the nature of elemental energy. What this means is that you must embrace Creation so you can benefit from it. Remember, you are taking this journey to be transformed into your true self. It is a time when your intellectual vision and your spiritual perceptions will take the lead role to guide you to greater wisdom about divine law.

The basic fallacy believed by many about connecting with Divinity is that only a select few have the ability to do so! While it is true that not everyone will make the divine connection, it's not because they don't have the ability to do so; it's that they prefer not to! The divine energy source is deep within you; in fact it is centered in your core. The daunting part for some people is to activate what comes from within. It is fear that stops people from discovery. Once you control your fear, it will be easier for you to make the connection with divine sources. When fear comes, the first thing to do is breathe, and then visualize in a relaxed way things that come naturally, like breathing, which is second nature to us. Or think of a bird taking flight. All living things have natural instincts built into them. The same is true of Spirituality; it is built into you. It is the juice that gives you the faith to make the journey that your destiny calls to you.

Anyone who decides to go on a spiritual journey must expect major interior upheavals to happen. Everything from your thoughts, starting with how you think about human ideology, to your very foundation will change. You will learn to combine your

Consenting to the Journey

spiritual values and your intelligence in your initiatives. A good way to begin to know yourself is to sit in silence. This is how your true self breathes into you and how the Divine shapes your being and allows you to hold the center of your soul. In this sense your spiritual journey will become more intense and you will focus more on the path leading you to who you are meant to be. As the energy that surrounds you increases it will make you a person who is constantly evolving. You will be one who knows how to balance the forces of Nature with a newfound consciousness that transforms you into a conduit for higher energy.

All these changes that are occurring are positive for you. You are coming into your own spiritual power and becoming the master of your mind. This is an integral part of your development because it is how you gain self-knowledge and inner transformation. As a spiritual person you will instinctively know how to make better opportunities for yourself. This type of liberation is totally natural because it allows you simply to be yourself. This is the way to enlightenment and discovering your true individuality. The person who knows himself is one who knows they are superior, and yet they have nothing to prove. They are people who extend love and compassion,; just being in their presence you can feel their calming effect.

As a guide, I can tell you that as you explore your spirituality, you will find inspiration in your collaboration with divine law. Don't try to control what is happening to you, let Nature take its course. Those of you that are open to changes will evolve. You will become grounded and transformed into a higher being. As you continue your journey , slowly you will feel your energy rising. Your eyes will begin to open to the energies that join our world with higher dimensions. Your life is not determined by others or traditions. It is determined by your own energetic encounter that you will have with divine sources. Your spiritual well-being is an ongoing process; it doesn't stop because stopping is not possible with the Divine. As you learn to open up to divine sources, they will receive you. The transformation starts at your center and from there it spreads to your entire being. The experiences that will result are beyond what are considered daily occurrences. This is how you meet your very soul. If this sounds deep to you then your subconscious is expanding and you are moving towards enlightenment. Learn to see without any spiritual prejudice and you will meet your true self. Just let your consciousness glide into oneness with the divine energy that is calling you, and you will feel peace within. When this happens know you are close to the truth.

The best way to describe the results of the journey you are about to embark on is that you will find inner peace and greater stability. It will become essential that you make use of the energy that belongs to you. This will be a great source of motivation for you and it will allow you to accept everything that you are . Along the way, learn to appreciate everything for what it is in both the natural and supernatural realms. Focus on balancing your spiritual needs with how you live your daily life. When you choose to focus on the things that are positive, beauty grows you see as a divine being. This is your journey and you will find the illumination that you were born with. Just stay on the path and you will succeed!

Part II: Victory of the Soul
Living with Spiritual Abundance

The spiritual journey is beyond illusion in itself. Once on the journey all you need to do is let go and live it. Despite some blind spots that each of us face along the way, you will find your true being is an unstoppable force from within. The divine forces and natural elements take a leading role and guide you toward fulfillment. Anything that held you back or had you conditioned to disbelieve your capacity to become a divine being will fall away. You will finally know what is like to be at one with the universe and its forces. You will know abundance in all good things. Inner peace, love, and understanding will be yours, and you will finally be at one with the highest source of energy, the Creator of all Creation! Destiny is calling you to enter into the divine state and shut out all the noise that can sometimes fill your head. Set out confidently on your spiritual path and don't worry about the past. You can never go back in time; it is the present that holds your challenges.

You have nothing to lose and everything to gain. Soar on your adventure, because you are about to cross a threshold in your mind. Now is the time to ask the Divine all your questions, , because the present moment holds an infinite number of possibilities. Embrace your spirituality with gratefulness, and you will begin to manifest your dreams. When your true being joins together with Divinity you are creating a shift of mind, body, and spirit. Be constant and methodical in your approach. Keep perfecting the rituals that you are learning so you can unite your consciousness with the Divine. The changes that result will lead to a renewal of your spirit. You will be free to better understand the basis of universal life. Your inner force will grow tremendously and an unbreakable link will be formed with the Source of Creation. This marks a time when you inner being will be fed abundantly and a luminous light will fill you. All things are now possible for you. A strong passion for the truth impels you on your spiritual quest to discover your place on Earth. By opening yourself up to your divine purpose you

Explore Your Sacred Truth

are aiding your higher awareness to blossom. This stage is called "the grid," referring to the power of sacred geometry within that holds the key to your inner being. You are at the turning point of your life where free-flowing energy on every level ties together all you are learning into complete spiritual harmony. Enjoy what is happening to you and allow yourself to embrace what it has to offer to you. I said in an earlier chapter that you are the seed and the Source of Creation is the manifestation. You will have the power of seeing beyond what is known, This is all part of your journey. Live it, breathe it, and most of all absorb it; your life is charting a new course for you. Bring all these lessons you have learned into your everyday world. It will make the difference between living an ordinary life or living the ultimate sacred unity.

Spiritual abundance is fed to you from Divine Creation. This is ancient wisdom that has always been available for human beings to access. For centuries this wisdom was hidden from most, but now there is a shift occurring, in which you are being called to learn that you are the sole owner of your vision. It is up to you to respond to the call so you may raise your vibration. Once you are receptive to it the mind can cannot break away from the journey. As a guide I say to you, live your life in awareness because that is the way out of the depths that can stop your growth. Now is the time to use the creative energy that the Divine is offering you. This gift will allow you to blossom and grow in ways you have only imagined up until now.

You will be inspired to keep on and you will attain the power to reach spiritual purity. You will become thirsty for your own life experiences, not those of anyone else. This is your path and it is filled with mysticism and lightheartedness. This path calms both physical and emotional suffering, leading you to rise to a greater level of consciousness. The vulnerability that may have once plagued you will no longer exist. Your life should be an inquiry into who you are; everything else is secondary. This is the only way to make a true connection with the divine energy. This is the only way to become whole and a complete higher being. Everything ties together when you use spiritual intelligence with an intellectual approach. You should dedicate time each day to connect from within and keep the portal to higher dimensions open. Become one with the universe and the Divine because that is the way that you connect with higher realms. The rituals you've learned will help you to achieve in ways you never would have thought possible. This is your time for renewal and the changes that will reorient your life. Using your spiritual intelligence you can become the image that you create. You are one of billions on Earth. Each person is unique. Your life has meaning. Learn to become as a current of water and flow in the direction that is your own.

Think of spiritual freedom as the end to a stagnating period in your life, bringing inspiration to your being. This change, should you decide to make it, will give you the opportunity to live in a non-superficial world in which creative energy enables you to perform at your best any task that comes your way. Detach yourself from anything that mentally holds you back so you may fulfill your journey. Whether you are aware of it or not , your soul is being filled with a spiritual energy that is charting a new road for you. This will have an incredibly favorable impact on your life and change your current views.

Spiritual intelligence is the knowledge we acquire through our own experiences. It enables us to make intelligent decisions instead of those that have been conditioned by tradition. It is through spiritual intelligence that you enter into what is called by many the dawn of humanity. To enter this state, the key rule is you must know your true self. Then, like the pieces of a puzzle, it all begins to fit together. There are no boundaries once you let go and embrace the Divine. Once you do so it will lead you to a life of meaning. In these times, so many people feel lost. They do not realize that there is a way to live a balanced and happy life.

I invite you to explore the alternatives that spirituality has to offer you and experience the divine journey for yourself. Only then can you decide with intelligence what is right for you. You are a soul with unlimited potential and numerous possibilities before you. Trust your inner being to guide you to receiving the gifts the divine energies and the universe are offering you. You are the only one that can find the truth of your being. Even though the pilgrimage may be long, you'll realize your true nature, the essence of your existence, and achieve a new awareness free from illusions.

The spiritual purification you are going through is the prelude to an inner transformation that will lead to the liberation of your soul. This is the path to an new social and spiritual balance that will bestow on you an internal harmony. When you create balance in your life, you also create peace and access the power of the Now. This is how you rid your psyche of any contaminated elements that have prevented you from turning on your inner light. It is time for you to embrace the changes and transformations. This means that the outside world and your subconscious will merge with the laws of the universe. You will be in what is called "full flow," fully feeling the universe and its energy. This is a positive experience of divine energy that you will access. The journey will teach you wisdom that deepens your aptitudes in the spiritual realms and shows you your unique place on Earth.

Consenting to the Journey

THE LIGHT FROM WITHIN

Every human soul has an inner light that is waiting to be brought to the surface. You are the only one who can will your own spiritual change. Show no resistance to the Divine, and the Creator of all energy will disclose to you the hidden knowledge you need to access the light you have within. Each person on this planet sees the world differently; you must learn to view the landscape that is meant for you. When you do, you open a portal to the divine awareness that is in you. This is a beautiful clarity for your soul. Let the silence be your teacher, and your inner guide will direct you.

Your soul has infinite depth. When I speak of releasing the light within, I am guiding you to discover your hidden knowledge. This will show you how to use wisdom and respect, and will be an ally for you in interactions with other humans. By accessing the light that comes from within, you will be able to show compassion, develop disciple, and let the Divine unfold in you. By allowing the flow of divine energy to enter your life, you master your future. You've heard it said, 'Don't let the flow pass you by because the same flow never passes by twice.' Let yourself flow like the Nature that surrounds you. Each day it is fresh. If you take notice before old foliage falls away, new buds are already forming. Such is the same with your light; it is nonstop. You must not be intimidated by this side of life because with it comes a deep human and spiritual satisfaction.

The smallest changes and adjustments that sometimes go unnoticed are making life-changing transformations for your benefit. Remember you are surrounded by the divine realm, and when you look at yourself from within you awaken your true nature. There are no masks when you achieve true spirituality.

Explore Your Sacred Truth

The reward is that you no longer question why you are here; you know. The stresses of these times have less of an effect on you .

From birth most of us are conditioned into thinking that what is taught to us is the truth. When you discover the path to awareness and use your intelligence, it opens up your intellect. You'll discover that truth depends on the individual seeking it. This discovery opens new possibilities for you. It helps you to see your value in the world without fear. Use this time to reflect on your purpose and to learn about your soul by connecting with the divine life forces that surround you. This is how you keep your faith and spirit shining bright.

There comes a times where all you have learned is implemented in your daily living. Breathe deeply and let awareness enter into your being. Your are receiving a unique gift from the Divine that will allow you to see past the veil of the ordinary and enter a world in which you begin to understand that your soul has meaning and you are not just passing through this life without hope. There is a mission that you must fulfill.

The road which you will now take is leading you towards spiritual fulfillment and human happiness. Take this opportunity to fully develop your spiritual side and use the knowledge you have acquired to have continued harmony in your life. Follow the path that is meant for you and live your life according to your own truth. For centuries man has been trying to figure out what the purpose of life is, never stopping to appreciate that the fundamentals are encoded in their DNA and the answers are within them. The beyond is opening its gates to you . Be ready to accept what the mysteries of life have to offer you. It is time to devote your energy to better organizing your life . If you allow it, your spirit can take you far. Remember the spiritual journey is personal and has nothing to do with religion. It is about discovering and living in your true being. There are new beginnings ahead for you. Once you commit yourself to the Divine, new perspectives will open up for you and you will see things the way they really are. Expanding your gifts not only benefits you but also others that are put in your path. Within you are many hidden gifts that are waiting to be brought to the surface. Stay grounded and focused and the Divine will help you uncover what lies within you. It is up to you to make the decision to live in the light from within.

BECOME THE DIAMOND IN THE LOTUS

When I think of the lotus, I equate it with the true self. It is my favorite flower, not only for its beauty but for its symbolic meaning. The lotus is the only flower that grows in the mud and transforms from the dark depths to brilliancy—something like you on the spiritual journey you are taking. There will be times that you will question and doubt your path but as you continue forward the light of your inner being will shine like a diamond. You will be able to amass energy that will grow in you and enable you to reach new spiritual levels. You are inheriting the tools that are called wisdom, understanding, peace, and love. Most of all, you are coming to know acceptance of yourself.

When I was divinely inspired to write this book it was to help guide and teach you about the differences that each person may encounter on their journey. No two people are the same and no two roads to enlightenment are the same. The purpose of spirituality is to be able to accept responsibility for who you are and live your life to the fullest on your journey. No one ever said that the road to balance is always easy. Among the most spiritual people are the ones who have been tested the most. Do not be afraid of what is offered to you because you have been chosen by the Divine to participate in this journey.

Explore Your Sacred Truth

The goal of this book is to explain how to develop from within and to inspire you to move forward toward your destination. Everything that you are searching for spiritually will take place in its natural time. Any contradictions or complexities you may encounter along the way, you will overcome, and the result will be a great satisfaction to you. Divine forces are so much more powerful than worldly ones. You will live in the world but you will not be concerned with worldly things. You will have everything you need because the universe will provide it for you.

As you enter the state of awareness, suddenly you'll find that your thought process changes and you have access to a new knowledge that is divinely guided. Your inspiration will lead you toward spiritual glory and guide you in finding your soul. It is the direction of renewal and hope. You will learn how to awaken the ancient wisdom that is encoded in you but was asleep. The very core of your soul is the very life of your existence. Both you and the Divine have to meet in order to merge with one another. This is fundamental to becoming whole. Your inner energy force will be impressive and it will lead you to live your destiny.

You are the lotus, you are unique and unattached, you move inwards. You are becoming a divine being of light. The shift is powerful; it's opening the center of your energy flow. This is called self-empowerment; it is a gift from the Divine for you to use. You will be able to envisage clearly where divine direction is taking you. Your nature will become pure and, like the lotus, you will remained untouched in all you do.

As a being of light your presence is needed here. You have much to offer this planet, whether you realize it or not. You are being guided by the Divine and the Creator of all source energy to play a leading role to inducing change. Your guides will be working with you to show you the path that leads to communicating with the unseen worlds. This is how you will be able to expand your intuition. All is leading you towards a new life and new energy. You have a mission to accomplish and you will do it. Your mission is to find your inner soul and live your life on earth with positivity. Use the lessons and rituals throughout the book as tools to help you attain sacred truth.

The human psyche has many layers to it. Most people never discover the dynamics of their nature. By placing your trust in the Divine you are actively taking a stand for finding your true purpose. You have freed yourself from conditioning and are using spiritual intelligence as your guide. You are an exceptional being with divine power within to live with godly intellect. It is time to use it for your well-being. Do so with confidence and watch what will be offered to you. I simply say to you that you are a diamond in the lotus. Develop yourself to your fullest potential and live your own sacred truth. The Divine is calling you. Whatever you do, don't miss this calling. The river never flows the same way twice. You are a true being of light. Blessed be!

CPSIA information can be obtained
at www.ICGtesting.com
Printed in the USA
LVOW12s0911101217
559284LV00002B/405/P

9 781936 940561